Why Me, Lord?
Finding Joy in Affliction

Reginald Alexander

TEACH Services, Inc.
P U B L I S H I N G
www.TEACHServices.com • (800) 367-1844

World rights reserved. This book or any portion thereof may not be copied or reproduced in any form or manner whatever, except as provided by law, without the written permission of the publisher, except by a reviewer who may quote brief passages in a review.

The author assumes full responsibility for the accuracy of all facts and quotations as cited in this book. The opinions expressed in this book are the author's personal views and interpretations, and do not necessarily reflect those of the publisher.

This book is provided with the understanding that the publisher is not engaged in giving spiritual, legal, medical, or other professional advice. If authoritative advice is needed, the reader should seek the counsel of a competent professional.

Copyright © 2024 Reginald Alexander
Copyright © 2024 TEACH Services, Inc.
ISBN-13: 978-1-4796-1768-5 (Paperback)
ISBN-13: 978-1-4796-1769-2 (ePub)
Library of Congress Control Number: 2024903221

Scripture references marked (AMP) are taken from the Amplified Bible, copyright © 2015 by The Lockman Foundation, La Habra, CA 90631. Used by permission. All rights reserved.

Scripture references marked (ASV) are taken from the American Standard Version of the Bible. Public domain.

Scripture references marked (ERV) are taken from the Easy-to-Read Version of the Bible, copyright © 2006 by Bible League International.

Scripture quotations marked (ESV) are taken from The Holy Bible, English Standard Version. ESV® Text Edition: 2016. Copyright © 2001 by Crossway Bibles, a publishing ministry of Good News Publishers.

Scripture quotations marked (KJV) are taken from King James Version. Public domain.

Scripture references marked (NCV) are taken from The Holy Bible, New Century Version®, copyright © 2005 by Thomas Nelson, Inc. Used by permission.

Scripture quotations marked (NET) are taken from the NET Bible® copyright ©1996, 2019 by Biblical Studies Press, L.L.C. http://netbible.com Used by permission. All rights reserved.

Scripture quotations marked (NKJV) are taken from the New King James Version®. Copyright © 1982 by Thomas Nelson. Used by permission. All rights reserved.

All Scripture references marked (NIV) are taken from the Holy Bible, New International Version®, NIV®, copyright © 1973, 1978, 1984, 2011 by Biblica, Inc.®. Used by permission. All rights reserved worldwide.

Scripture quotations marked (NKJV) are taken from the New King James Version®. Copyright © 1982 by Thomas Nelson. Used by permission. All rights reserved.

Scripture quotations marked (NLT) are taken from Holy Bible, New Living Translation, copyright © 1996, 2004. 2015 by Tyndale House Foundation. Used by permission of Tyndale House Publishers, Inc., Carol Stream, Illinois 60188. All rights reserved.

Published by

TEACH Services, Inc.
P U B L I S H I N G
www.TEACHServices.com • (800) 367-1844

Dedication

This book is dedicated from a heart of love to all the hurting heroes still on the journey of affliction. You have decided to keep moving forward in the struggle and have not given up. I salute you for your bravery.

I wrote this book with you in mind. I have discovered that experiencing affliction can be challenging, especially when the pain seems unbearable. It can evoke a wide range of emotions and leave one in a confused mental state, crying out, "Why me, Lord?!" You (or someone you know) may be in that place right now. You may be seeking comfort, or want to encourage someone else. Take heart, child of God!

Remember you and your loved ones are not alone. Our heavenly Father is with you in Jesus Christ, His Son, through the Spirit of the Living God. Because of Their divine presence dwelling in your heart, your affliction does not define you as broken and hopeless. You can find true joy and divine purpose in your affliction, as I have experienced in my suffering. Continue to trust the Lord's endless wisdom in your grief even while seeking the answer to the question, "Why me, Lord?"

Table of Contents

Foreword: Prayer for the Reader vii

Special Thanks viii

Introduction 9

I Want to Live 13

Can I Live a Full Life? 16

The Goodness of the Lord 19

What about Our Children? 22

The Triple-Braided Cord 25

Planning for Widowhood 28

Aching Heart 31

I'm Overwhelmed 34

Trust in the Lord 37

Setback 40

One Hug Will Do 43

Life in Songs	46
A Soldier's Testimony: Ms. Wharton	49
Power in God's Word	52
The Second Interview	55
Heavenly Atmosphere	58
Struggle to Pray	61
Don't Worry	64
I Have a Question	67
3 A.M.	70
When My Voice Was Silent	73
Dark Shell	76
Cardiac Arrest	79
How Long, Lord	82
Bound!	85
Come On, Dad. You Can Do This!	88
Encouragement in the Foxhole	91
Wisdom in Season	94
Purpose in Brokenness	97
Reflections	100

Prayer for the Reader

*L*ord, we give thanks unto you for breathing life into our lungs and granting us liberty and salvation through your beloved Son. May we continue to look towards the hills from whence cometh our strength, keeping our eyes and focus upon the Lord, casting all matters of care upon the shoulders of the Lord. Although life may place us on a rollercoaster ride of affliction, taking us through many hurdles and challenges in life, may we hold fast to your faith and trust in You, which gives us the strength and perseverance to carry on!

Dear reader, may God's will be done and may it be sufficient in your life, enriching your heart with His love, His joy, and the everlasting peace of Christ that His miraculous power of healing may be shown mighty in your life, drawing you closer to the heart of God, bringing you complete restoration in the mighty name of Jesus Christ.

Sincerely,
Moore Faith
Sarcoidosis Survivor

Special Thanks

To my mother, Ethel Alexander. There's nothing like a mother's comfort. We praise God for you, Mom—for showers of comfort seasoned with grace, love, and compassion full of mercy. Your children and your grandchildren know the journey has not always been easy for you as a single parent, but you never stopped caring for us—even in your affliction and when we did not deserve your love. Thank you, Jesus! Bless His holy name. I praise God for my mother, Ethel Alexander, also known as Grandma Sissy. May the Lord comfort you in this life's travel. In Jesus' name. Amen.

To my home conference, the Allegheny East Conference of Seventh-day Adventists, and its members for the financial and spiritual support I received, visits on the weekends, and meeting others' needs. I praise God for each and every one of you.

To my colleagues fighting heart failure alongside me on the fifth floor of Johns Hopkins Hospital in Baltimore—in the foxhole trying to stay alive. Your emotional support, companionship, and understanding meant so much to me. Thank you, David Doidge, Julie Buck, Lisa Smith, and Louise Pontillo, just to name a few. Much love.

To all my family and friends, I appreciate your prayers and words of encouragement on my journey of affliction. I'm forever grateful.

Introduction

In this book, you will notice that in the middle of every chapter, the story is interrupted with "BREAKING NEWS!" This is where the narrative shifts gears from the crisis to finding hope by allowing the gospel to speak to your suffering and lead you to experience joy in affliction. Each chapter ends with a rededication prayer.

I encourage you to read the chapters of this book in order without skipping around. The journey described in this book begins with a life-threatening health crisis in July 2017, and ends with my return home nineteen months later after extreme medical intervention. At the end of the book, additional devotional reflections will inspire you to keep moving in your physical, emotional, and mental affliction and will remind you that you are still valuable in God's eyes. You have much to offer your family, the suffering in society, and Jesus Christ.

Why Me, Lord? Finding Joy in Affliction, began long before my health crisis. Let's take a look back at my journey. June 2006 was an exciting time for me, my wife, and our seven-year-old son. We had just accepted a full-time call to the Publishing Ministry Department of the Allegheny East Conference (AEC) of the Seventh-day Adventist Church. There I would work with pastors in the Washington, D.C. metro area. You may think that such a position meant that I was an expert in writing and publishing books. That was not the case.

Immediately before accepting that call, we were living in one of the marriage dorms at Oakwood College (now Oakwood University). Oakwood is a Seventh-day Adventist institution of higher learning and a historically

Black university located in Huntsville, Alabama. I was pursuing a four-year degree in theology with a little over two and a half years left to go. However, the classes were becoming more and more challenging for me and I was having a hard time doing the work. In spring of 2006, shortly after coming off academic probation, I flunked out of college! I had succumbed to my dyslexia. My twin brother Angelo and I have struggled with writing, reading, and math since our early educational years. One time, in elementary school, the administrators encouraged my mother to pull us out of school. They believed we couldn't learn academic subjects.

Lack of educational training in certain subjects from my early years, combined with not receiving the proper learning skills, made college work extremely hard.

It did not appear that I would enter the ministry. However, the Lord was faithful in fulfilling the vision He gave me–just in another way I didn't expect. Attending Oakwood College was a miracle in and of itself, but when all odds were against me I received, and by God's grace, answered, the call to ministry. What seems impossible to man, is all possible to God! Thank you, Jesus!

After my first year in the ministry, the Lord allowed me to start a vibrant student literature evangelist missionary program called "Youth 4 Change." This ministry was composed of high school and college students. During school breaks, the students would work to raise money for their Christian schooling. The students went door-to-door and parking lot to parking lot selling kids' books, health materials, and adult devotionals. They would also gather names of people interested in receiving Bible studies and other life-enhancing resources. We averaged between fifteen and twenty student missionaries at a time. The ministry grew each year, and I had big dreams of seeing it thrive.

However, in January 2016, those dreams came to a screeching halt. I began experiencing physical symptoms that affected my work. Over the next three years, I experienced:

- respiratory issues
- fluid buildup around the lungs
- chronic fatigue
- an enlarged heart

- AFib (fast, abnormal heart rate)
- low cardiac output
- very low ejection fraction

My emotional symptoms included:

- depression
- anxiety
- fear
- sadness
- hopelessness

The psychological struggles led me to cry out in grief:

- Why me, Lord?!
- I don't understand!
- Where are You, Lord?
- Lord, do you care?

This health crisis had me under tremendous stress and in deep pain. However, the Lord graciously brought me through. Bless His holy name! I am forever grateful.

Struggle is still a real part of my life. I face ongoing health challenges. I strive to function in spite of my extreme dyslexia. I daily battle with writing, reading, and correctly pronouncing words in my ministry—but that is a testimony for another book. My journey continues.

I pray that through this book you will experience life-changing inspiration and insights, and that you will discover your purpose in suffering while waiting for healing and deliverance in this life. Even more important, if the healing or the release from your affliction doesn't come as you expect, I hope this book helps you remain faithful in your affliction until your final deliverance from sin, sickness, and sorrow at the second coming of our Lord and Savior, Jesus Christ!

I.
I Want To Live

Under a clear blue sky, with close to ninety degree weather, on July 9, 2017, at 12:30 p.m., I was at the Washington National Zoo with my family. It was there I found myself waking up on the ground with a face hovering over me and a voice asking: "Are you okay?"

"Yes, I don't know what exactly happened," I said, confused, as I tried to reason within myself.

A few seconds later, the same voice, which was that of a surgeon, told me, "You passed out."

I did not realize at that moment that my heart was going out. I was experiencing a heart attack, a life-threatening event caused by ventricular tachycardia (VT), which is an abnormally fast heart rate that begins in the lower chamber of the heart and affects the action of the chamber that sends oxygenated blood to the body. Because my heart was beating so fast, my body organs were not able to receive oxygenated blood, causing me to faint.

Wow! I passed out!

"Are you dehydrated?" the doctor asked.

"No, I don't think so," I replied. "I'm a heart failure patient."

By this time, I was sitting up against my wife's back.

> **Don't let me die in front of my wife and kids!**
> **I want to live.**

Within a few minutes, the doctor shouted, "He's passing out again! Lay him down. Lift his legs. Pour some water over his face. We need to shade his face from the sun!"

Moaning and groaning, I couldn't speak. My legs were moving; my body was hot.

Lord, I'm so scared! Please keep me! I cried out in my heart, as I shed a few tears. *Don't let me die in front of my wife and kids! I want to live.*

BREAKING NEWS!

David declares: "The Lord hears his people when they call to him for help. He rescues them from all their troubles. The Lord is close to the brokenhearted; he rescues those whose spirits are crushed" (Ps. 34:17, 18, NLT).

What David expressed was my understanding of God, remembering who He is and what He could do in my dilemma when I prayed. While lying there on the ground, I was wrestling with the thought, *Will He get me out of this?* I recognized that I knew He could, and I believed in His power to deliver me. But, would He have mercy on me? I knew I could die if it were His will. *But Lord, I want to live!*

Yet, beneath the uncertainty and the fear of whether I would live or die, I continued holding on—with all my might and through the prayer of faith—to the promises of God. I was trying to stay calm, knowing that doing so was my only chance of survival. My only hope was that God hears and answers prayers.

My hope through prayer strengthened me in my affliction as death was near. Says the psalmist, when they call to Him for help, "He rescues them from all their troubles" (Ps. 34:17, NLT).

Wounded warrior, child of God—

Be encouraged. As difficult as it can be to find yourself fighting for your life—when all else fails—hold onto Him with all your might. When you have no control over the situation to save yourself, do not stop praying! Pray the prayer of faith, trusting God until you offer up your last breath and close your eyes in Christ. Remember, you have a Heavenly Father who does hear and answer prayers. He is still in the life-saving business.

God's promise: "The eyes of the LORD are upon the righteous, and his ears are open unto their cry" (Ps. 34:15, KJV).

Prayer

El Roi—the God who sees me,

I am moving forward in my afflictions by God's grace, utilizing the weapon of prayer in wartime—especially when the fear of death is nearby. I will call out to You for deliverance and for help, grabbing hold of your strength from the heart of faith through prayer till triumph is given or till I offer up my last breath.

Knowing that, when I call You for help, I have the possibility that my request may get answers when all else fails. Also, I would like to thank You, Lord, for all those You have sent to help me stay alive on my journey by Your Holy Spirit. I appreciate their service, Lord. You are my Helper. I trust entirely in You.

I give You my will.
In the victorious holy name of Jesus Christ. Amen.

2.

Can I Live A Full Life?

Following the attack at the zoo, I was taken to the fifth floor of Johns Hopkins Hospital. My wife was in the room, and I was lying in bed physically and emotionally exhausted. My health was unstable, and my cognitive level was low.

I was recovering from a heart rate of 217 bpm. This caused me to faint at the zoo. During that time, the doctors shared that I was hit with the VT attack, which caused me to pass out. My heart was still unstable. They were trying to get it back to a safe rhythm.

I didn't have much to say to the doctors and nurses walking in and out of the room. I was out of it mentally and physically. I listened to my wife arguing with the doctor, seeking answers. She was confused, frustrated, and scared.

What caused this attack and my failing heart over the past year and a half? There was a void of answers and only speculation.

"We don't know right now, but cardiac sarcoidosis could have caused it. We need to run some tests."

Sarcoidosis—what was that? Is it cancerous? Can I live a full life with it? *Lord, I'm worried!*

BREAKING NEWS!

"For our light and momentary troubles are achieving for us an eternal glory that far outweighs them all. So we fix our eyes not on what is seen, but on what is unseen, since what is seen is temporary, but what is unseen is eternal" (2 Cor. 4:17, 18, NIV).

After I heard the doctor's report, survival mode kicked in. I was not thinking about anyone but myself. Was I being selfish? I didn't feel that I was. The thought that I might die in a few weeks or months from sarcoidosis while everyone else's life continued was profoundly disappointing. *I will become a memory that fades away as time passes*, I thought.

To stay positive, I thought more about heaven and the amazing things the Lord has in store for me there when I enter those pearly gates at His second coming. I fixed my eyes "not on what is seen, but on what is unseen, since what is seen is temporary, but what is unseen is eternal" (2 Cor. 4:18, NIV).

Promises like this revolutionized my broken spirit, pumping life into my heart and counteracting my fear. Anxiety and frustration removed their negative impact on my emotional being. This gave me hope and something to look forward to as a child of God if I was laid to rest before my time. The journey with sarcoidosis would be short compared to the eternal journey. *Yes, Lord!* Within forty-eight hours, the doctor walked into the room with the report, "Reg, we ran the tests for cardiac sarcoidosis. You tested positive. It's running down the center of your heart."

Wounded warrior, child of God—

When sickness or tragedy brings the fear of death, with all of your might by God's grace, turn away from focusing on the crisis, which will only last for a short season in your tears of anguish. Instead, turn to focus on the eternal place and rest your mind there. I call it sweet heaven, where there's no more pain, hurt, or sickness. It will have a tremendous impact on your emotional and spiritual state of health, lifting it out of the pit of despair. You will find joy in your affliction even when thoughts of death are present.

God's promise: "For our citizenship is in heaven, from which we also eagerly wait for the Savior, the Lord Jesus Christ, who will transform our lowly body that it may be conformed to His glorious body" (Phil. 3:20, 21, NKJV).

Prayer

El Roi, the God who sees me—

Thank You, Lord, for that beautiful place You have prepared for me in heaven where You live. I will no longer have to live with pain and sickness or take any more daily medication with side effects. And the suffering of this life in all its forms will cease.

Lord, help me to become consumed with this thought about heaven daily and its wonderful blessings that are waiting for me there to enjoy so I can experience peace now in my affliction even when I'm scared and when the situation seems so dark and hopeless, not knowing what the outcome will be until I reach that heavenly paradise, knowing something better waits for me on the other side of life.

I give You my will.

In the victorious holy name of Jesus Christ. Amen.

3.

The Goodness of the Lord

Months after my VT attack, Elder Paulin Phillips asked me to give a testimony about the goodness of the Lord in sparing my life there at the zoo. The attack almost took my life, and I had a testimony. Therefore, on Sabbath morning, I was at the Columbia Community Center Seventh-day Adventist Church in Columbia, Maryland, along with a few others, testifying about God's goodness in our suffering and how He brought us through.

After the preliminaries were over, the testimonies began. I was the first to share. I was excited for the opportunity as it was my first speaking engagement since the attack. I was a little nervous as I made my way to the podium, fearing I might not do a good job. My body and mind were under stress. My heart was still very weak from the attack, and I had lost a significant amount of weight. I struggled with my memory, but my iPad helped me recall the five miracles that took place that day. I was feeling anxious. My body was hot, and I began to sweat. I felt I shouldn't be doing this. I cried out in my mind, *Lord, please get me through this testimony!*

BREAKING NEWS!

"But I will sing of thy power; yea, I will sing aloud of thy mercy in the morning: for thou hast been my defence and refuge in the day of my trouble. Unto thee, O my strength, will I sing: for God is my defence, and the God of my mercy" (Ps. 59:16, 17, KJV).

I began to share the story of God's protecting hand over my life in the past year and a half, along with the events that led up to the day of the VT attack. I had experienced complete heart blockage and an enlarged heart, with only ten to twenty percent of my heart functioning. While telling my story, I was excited. My strength was being renewed as I shared my testimony about God's wonderful protecting grace over my family and life. God kept us, not allowing the VT attack to occur on the highway while I was traveling down I-32, I-95, and I-495 to the zoo. The attack hit me inside the zoo—just one minute after getting off the road and parking the vehicle.

I heard choruses of "Hallelujah!" and "Amen!" echoing throughout the sanctuary. I was on cloud nine and didn't want to finish testifying about His mighty power sparing our lives on the highway. However, my time was up, and I realized all anxiety had left me. So I concluded with the passage from Psalm 59:16, 17, KJV. Energy and passion were bubbling up from the depths of my soul as I acknowledged the fullness of God's grace to me in my affliction. "Yea, I will sing aloud of Thy mercy ... for Thou hast been my defense and refuge in the day of my trouble ... O my strength, will I sing."

Wounded warrior, child of God—

In your affliction, push through whatever challenges you're facing, testifying of His delivering power, leaving out no details from whatever crisis has left you wounded and feeling hopeless. Name your blessings one by one without any hesitation. In doing so, you will find strength and your spirit will be lifted above your grief, pain, and suffering, making a difference in your life. So, go ahead and tell of His delivering acts. You can do this with God's help. You will experience joy in affliction.

God's promise: "For I can do everything through Christ, who gives me strength" (Phil. 4:13, NLT).

Prayer

El Roi, the God who sees me—

Lord, help me to not keep silent but to push through physical challenges with Your strength. Take away the fear of not doing an excellent job when I am given the opportunity to testify about Your goodness in my affliction. Thank You for sparing my life and the life of my family from any tragic events from the devil's attack.

You deserve honor and praise for who You are—the One full of mercy and grace who looks beyond my faults to supply me with safety, deliverance, and protection. Keep me, Lord, through Your never-failing love and everlasting compassion, for I realize that I cannot keep myself on this journey of affliction.

I give You my will.
In the victorious holy name of Jesus Christ. Amen.

4.

What About Our Children?

My health crisis continued. My daily hustle and bustle of fighting heart failure to stay alive was caused by a life-threatening autoimmune inflammatory disease called sarcoidosis, which can shorten the life of those who contract it. Taking multiple pills daily and experiencing side effects of those medications was becoming exhausting. I was battling depression, anxiety, and fatigue. Hospital visits and ongoing cardiac rehab were beyond tiring. *Mercy, Lord, when will this thing come to an end?*

It was causing me to worry more about the future and the safety of my two little girls, Eden and Brooke. What if I passed away and my wife married a crazy nut who would take advantage of them sexually? What if they find themselves experiencing emotional and sociologically abusive relationships that they may find challenging to get out of? Who will help them if I'm not there?

I wrestled with the thought that there may be a possibility of not being around to encourage, protect, and navigate my girls through this dangerous world. What if I don't live long enough to see them become respectable God-fearing young ladies? These feelings of uncertainty brought on depression and anxiety, leaving me feeling emotional and causing me great grief.

Lord, help me, please! I'm overwhelmed with constant sorrow!

BREAKING NEWS!

"The earth is the Lord's, and the fulness thereof; the world, and they that dwell therein" (Ps. 24:1, KJV).

Who has the primary role of provider, protector, encourager, and caregiver over the lives of my children if I happen to die from cardiac sarcoidosis before my time?

"You act like their lives are depending on you, Reg. Stop worrying about all that. The Lord can take care of your girls far better than you can, whether you're dead or alive!"

This word was from my father in ministry, Elder William Smith, Publishing Director of the Southern Union of Seventh-day Adventists, who shared encouraging words that lifted my spirit in my affliction. When these concerns invaded my mind a few months after my VT attack, his words of spiritual wisdom caused me to reflect on Scripture passages like Psalm 24:1, KJV.

"The earth is the LORD's, and the fulness thereof; the world, and they that dwell therein."

Contemplating the Scriptures made me feel less worried and gave me a little more peace of mind regarding the future safety of my children. I was reminded that my girls are always under the domain and control of our Creator God. I relinquished these thoughts in pain and the feeling of responsibility that rested totally on me—even though it was not easy. I began to believe that things would work out okay. This realization made a big difference in moving forward in trusting God to take care of them. The burden was gradually being lifted. I was finding joy in my affliction.

> *Contemplating the Scriptures made me feel less worried and gave me a little more peace of mind regarding the future safety of my children.*

Wounded warrior, child of God—

Be encouraged and continue to trust Christ when you find yourself wrestling with these negative thoughts regarding the future safety of your children in your absence. Refocus! Pray this prayer:

Our Heavenly Father, [Adonai] ... Lord of all, You can take care of our children far better than we can, whether we're alive or dead, because, ultimately, they are Yours. You have them in the palm of your hands. Lord, keep our children safe even if we die before our time, and save them in Your eternal kingdom. Amen!

God's promise: "Defend the poor and fatherless; Do justice to the afflicted and needy. Deliver the poor and needy; Free them from the hand of the wicked" (Ps. 82:3

Prayer

El Roi, the God who sees me—

Please help me trust You, knowing that You will take care of my family and the children that You have entrusted to me here on earth if I am laid to rest before my time.

In those distressing times, bring back to my mind that You are far more interested in their well-being, safety, and salvation than I am. Would You please help me relinquish control as the protector while I still do my part to care for them and place them now in Your hands? I want to be liberated from this fear of the unknown and live in the spirit of optimism about their future because they are Yours.

I give You my will.

In the victorious holy name of Jesus Christ. Amen.

5.

The Triple-Braided Cord

A few months had passed since I shared my testimony at the Columbia Seventh-day Adventist Church in March. My health seemed to have been improving, and my ejection fraction (EF) numbers increased my heart function from 10% to around 25–30%. A healthy heart EF is 55–65%. I was feeling much better physically. Psychologically and emotionally, I was optimistic about beating cardiac sarcoidosis.

I felt good! I hit LA Fitness daily, worked with a trainer, swam, lifted weights, and briskly walked on treadmills. Overall, my strength was being renewed. My diet had gone to a higher level through my juicing and consuming smoothies and 65% raw foods. And I was back on the preaching trail.

My twin brother, Angelo, who was living with me at the time, drove me throughout the Allegheny East Conference territory campaigning for an evangelistic project, "Hasten His Coming," which inspired members to invest financial resources—and themselves—into the publishing work to get literature out into the community. The project brought hope as it encouraged the people and created change as they got ready for the second coming of Christ.

But I wasn't out of the woods just yet!

BREAKING NEWS!

"A person standing alone can be attacked and defeated, but two can stand back-to-back and conquer. Three are even better, for a triple-braided cord is not easily broken" (Eccl. 4:12, NLT).

Around the beginning of May, I began to experience symptoms like I had experienced in the past: lightheadedness, dizziness, and lack of coordination behind the steering wheel. I would feel these before arriving or after leaving the gym. At home, the daily activity and chores around the house seemed to become more challenging, and they slowly reversed back to what life was like right after the attack. The shortness of breath and the fatigue were no longer improving. Depression and anxiety made their presence known, and I was operating out of pain and hurt, with little or no strength to care for my family.

My twin brother was there for our girls, providing daily support, nutrition, and hygiene. He took them to the playground, on daily walks and runs, and he played indoor and outdoor games with them. He fixed breakfast, lunch, and dinner and folded their clothes. My brother gave them baths and put them to bed at night and cared for the three-year-old grandson named Henry, whom he was raising at the time. He cleaned the house, moved things around that I couldn't lift, drove me to the store and different appointments, and so much more.

Under the weight of it all, I would have collapsed—maybe even died—defeated by cardiac sarcoidosis if my twin brother, along with his wife, had not been there for my wife and me. He was the third shoulder to lean on outside of my medical team, the third part of that "triple-braided cord." Indeed, he was a blessing. Through my brother's act of sacrifice in leaving Washington State to spend time with me for almost a year, I found joy in my affliction.

Wounded warrior, child of God—

Be encouraged and permit me to speak to your caregiver connected to you right now who is helping you stay alive. I salute you in your endeavor to care for your loved one who is wounded. I know the task can be challenging to your mental health and taxing to your physical body. Don't be afraid to ask for help. Find a shoulder (or two) to lean on "for a triple-braided cord is not easily broken" (Eccl. 4:12, NLT). Additionally, turn to God for help, the One who is the complete source of your strength. He will help you endure the hardship of functioning as a caregiver and He will strengthen you in your affliction.

God's promise: "My health may fail, and my spirit may grow weak, but God remains the strength of my heart; he is mine forever" (Ps. 73:26, NLT).

Prayer

El Roi, the God who sees me—

I must be honest—it is difficult as a caregiver to care for a sick spouse or for family members or friends while keeping a smile on my face and pep in my steps. Help me not to have a nervous breakdown in the trenches caring for my home, my kids or while working a full-time job. It's not easy.

Lord, can You send someone my way with a caring heart to help carry this heavy weight, or lead me to someone with a willing heart to help bear the load? Help me humble myself to be ready to release the task to the special person who is willing to help and to lean on You every step of the way.

I give You my will.

In the victorious holy name of Jesus Christ. Amen.

6.

Planning for Widowhood

After living in Pennsylvania for three months, my wife and I decided to leave our home in Odenton, Maryland, the early part of June 2018. This decision was first based on the condition of my health, which was deteriorating pretty fast. We weren't sure whether I would live beyond another year or two. A heart transplant was not on the radar. Second, if I died, my wife could take care of the kids independently as a single parent a little more comfortably in Pennsylvania than in the big city. Her job and the girl's school would be on the same campus, and our home would not be too far from the location.

It was during that time in Pennsylvania that the symptoms continued to get worse. We lived in a cabin on the campgrounds where my wife worked until we could find a home. I called the doctor's office daily, harassing them. I wasn't feeling great. I didn't know what in the world was going on. Out of stress and desperation, I reached out to one of our denomination's health institutions, Wildwood Health Center in Georgia, for help with the healing process. I was denied acceptance once they received my medical records, and I was told there was nothing they could do.

Lord, I need you!

BREAKING NEWS!

"Moreover, the law entered, that the offence might abound. But where sin abounded, grace did much more abound" (Rom. 5:20, KJV).

The battle continued, fighting symptoms of cardiac sarcoidosis. The doctors felt they were losing ground from the medication, and the pacemaker was no longer working to fix the problem of strengthening my heart. My cardiologist, Dr. Nisha Gilotra, asked me to come down for the right catheterization procedure to check my cardiac output. It was scheduled for August 8th.

Right-heart catheterization is a procedure in which the doctor inserts a small hollow tube into a pulmonary artery's main blood vessel through the right side of the patient's neck, traveling into the right side of the heart. This measures the blood pressure and how much pumping the blood permits in the patient's heart, which carries blood throughout the body.

The day had arrived, and my wife and I showed up. The process lasted for about thirty to forty-five minutes. When it was done, I was moved to the waiting room. My wife came in, and not long afterward, my doctor showed up with the report.

"Reg, your cardiac output [the blood flow of the heart] is pushing out two liters of blood per minute throughout the body. That's not good. The average should be four to seven liters of blood per minute." The doctor continued.

"Reg, sarcoidosis is running down the center of your heart. It has not spread throughout your body. That's good news. We need to consider a heart transplant while your organs are still in good enough condition. If you wait, sarcoidosis can spread throughout the body. It's only in your heart, but other organs will eventually become damaged because the heart is not pumping enough blood throughout the body, which would make it difficult for us to pursue a transplant."

Wow! I was a little discouraged that I would have to lose my original heart. However, I found joy in my affliction, seeing that God had withheld the sarcoidosis from spreading throughout my body and keeping my organs in good enough shape for a transplant. Had the sarcoidosis spread, it would have hindered the process of my having a second chance at life.

I cried inside with gratitude. "But where sin abounded"–the sin of the sickness of cardiac sarcoidosis–"grace did much more abound." I realized at that moment that God, through His mercy, was working in my favor.

Wounded warrior, child of God—

Stay hopeful in affliction. Behind every dark cloud, there is a silver lining you may not see. God has not forsaken you. His mercies are still active in your situation—even when it seems hopeless. Be patient and wait quietly until God shows you where He is working. There's more grace in your suffering than you realize. He has never stopped taking care of you, even in your grief. By God's grace, you will experience joy in your affliction.

God's promise: "It is of the LORD's mercies that we are not consumed, because his compassions fail not. They are new every morning: great is thy faithfulness" (Lam. 3:22, 23, KJV)

Prayer

El Roi, the God who sees me—

I praise You, Jesus, right now for Your presence. You have not left nor forsaken me in my suffering. You are here with me now, even if I don't feel Your presence. Your grace is moving in my hardships when everything seems to be hopeless.

I desire to walk in my affliction, claiming the promise that, where the sin of suffering abounds, Your grace abounds much more. Lord, please give me the patience I need to wait in hardship. Allow me to experience Your joy till I can see the silver lining in the dark cloud working in my favor because it is there. Gracious God, You are worthy to be praised.

I give You my will.

In the victorious holy name of Jesus Christ. Amen.

7.

Aching Heart

I was feeling a little fatigued and worn out. I had just driven two and a half hours from Pine Forge, Pennsylvania, to the DC Metro area. It was 7:30 on a lovely summer evening as I stepped out of the car at a Walmart. I noticed that my steps were not as fast as my mind was commanding. Quite worried, I wondered if I would make it to the front door. Praise God; I did make it.

After being in the store for 30 minutes, my steps began dragging and my breathing became difficult. I could barely carry the few light items I held in my hand. I had to get a shopping cart, which I struggled to push throughout the store. My spirit was becoming crushed. I observed the young, the middle-aged, and even the elderly getting around much easier and faster than I.

I decided to pay for my items and leave. Exiting the store, I began to creep toward my car, freely and slowly shedding tears. My symptoms reminded me of my failing heart. The enemy of my soul was telling me, "The Lord is not with you! You are not getting out of this one. Look at you–you're struggling."

Lord! I'm hurting!

BREAKING NEWS!

"They do not fear bad news [David says]; they confidently trust the LORD to care for them" (Ps. 112:7, NLT).

I was trying to hold back tears while moving towards my vehicle. It was Psalm 112:7 that the Lord brought to my mind. I repeated it to myself over and over again. It was changing my attitude for good! I feared no negative report. (The trouble was, I was having difficulty breathing; I was barely walking; and I was dealing with my failing heart.) I was reminded that the devil and his angels are liars, and the truth is not in them. The Lord can turn this helpless situation around. He takes care of me!

I must be honest. Before getting to my vehicle (my spirit still crushed), I wrestled with staying positive because my physical condition had remained the same. The struggle was real! The battle continued as I got into the car. I began repeating the passage from Psalm 112, applying it to my situation, "I fear no negative report … the Lord takes care of me."

I continued repeating this all the way to the hotel. I got out of the car, went up to the room, and stepped into the shower. Before I knew it, I found myself rejoicing in the Lord. I jumped out of the shower and made my way to bed. This was my prayer, "Thank you, Lord, for who You are, what You can do, and what You will do for me!"

I fell asleep, my spirit lifted above my aching heart.

Wounded warrior, child of God—

Be encouraged. Never stop rehearsing and believing in God's promises regarding your helpless situation. Tell yourself that God will take care of you even if your situation remains the same. Stay the course, be positive, and press on. Don't let one negative thought claim victory over your mind. He is there with you. He has your back. He will not leave you in your despair. You will find your spirit lifted over the sorrow and above a heart that hurts. Joy can come in the middle of affliction!

God's promise: "Death and life are in the power of the tongue, and those who love it will eat its fruit" (Prov. 18: 21, NKJV).

Prayer

El Roi, the God who sees me—

My Lord and Savior, in times of trouble, I find it challenging and difficult to remain positive in situations that seem not to be getting better but worse, when the negative thoughts that I am defeated settle in my mind as uttered by the devil and his angels.

Help me overcome them by grabbing hold of Your promises that speak of Your love and care for me. Help me to claim them over and over again in my mind till I feel Your presence resting over me. I accept his lie no longer. I'm claiming victory today in Christ, Lord! I surrender my will right now. I'm choosing to dare again trusting in You.

I give You my will.

In Jesus Christ's victorious holy name. Amen.

8.

I'm Overwhelmed

It was about a little over a month after the proper catheter procedure that I had been scheduled for a heart transplant interview at the end of September. Man! I could not wait! I had a little over three weeks left to go, and my symptoms were getting worse. I was feeling the impact of living with heart failure.

Daily living remained stressful, and my frustration increased while we were still living in a cabin. We had not found a permanent place as yet, though we had been in Pennsylvania a few months. These first few months were not easy. There was no kitchen, no personal space, and the air quality in the cabin was poor. We were consistently hot and sweaty in that place. I was dealing with two little girls all day while my wife was working from 9 to 5:30 pm. Our son, age nineteen, was sleeping on the other side of the room, and the girls were in bed with mommy and daddy.

My heart was failing, and health issues were weighing down our household. On top of these, my wife and I were having problems. I remember talking to my counselor one afternoon during the first week in September over the phone, telling her I didn't think I would make it to see the heart transplant interview at the end of the month.

Lord, I'm overwhelmed with fear and anxiety. I commit my life into Your hands!

BREAKING NEWS!

"I waited patiently for the LORD; and he inclined unto me, and heard my cry. He brought me up also out of an horrible pit, out of the miry clay . . . .

And he hath put a new song in my mouth, even praise unto our God" (Ps. 40:1–3, KJV).

Three days after the conversation with the counselor on Labor Day weekend, I got a call from my doctor's office.

"Reg, you need to come in so we can look you over. We want to make sure you're okay due to your excessive calls stating that your symptoms are getting worse."

I was excited about the news! Hoping they would admit me into the hospital, my wife and I packed up, jumped into a vehicle with the girls, and made our way toward downtown Baltimore, Maryland, and the Johns Hopkins Bridge clinic. We finally made it to the hospital check-in. The wait wasn't too long. The evaluation was over quickly. Shortly afterward, my nurse practitioner said, "Reg, you will be okay. We're sending you home. Hang in there until the end of the month heart transplant interview."

My spirits were crushed. My family and I exited the building to return to the vehicle, heading to see our son in Odenton, Maryland. We were two hours out when I received a phone call from the doctor's office.

"Reg, come back! We're going to start the interview early. We are not going to wait until the end of the month. Come back now!"

My spirit began to rejoice! This experience was creating a new song of the deliverance of praise, recognizing the goodness of God moving on my behalf. It delivered me from the horrible pit of death and brought me praise in my affliction.

Wounded warrior, child of God—

When you find yourself in a hopeless situation, and God shows up to rescue you because the pit you cannot pull yourselves out of is causing a heavy heart, don't wait until later to give Him the praise of thankfulness. You may rob yourself of experiencing happiness that flows from a grateful heart. At that very second, give Him praise and thank Him for His delivering act. The crisis you find yourself in right now God may be using to create a new song of praise that will make a difference in your despair, bringing you joy in affliction.

God's promise: "I will praise you, LORD, with all my heart; I will tell of all the marvelous things you have done. I will be filled with joy because of you. I will sing praises to your name, O Most High" (Ps. 9:1, 2, NLT).

Prayer

El Roi, the God who sees me—

I am sorry for not praising You when You have delivered me from situations in which I should have lost my life or mind. I was selfish and ungrateful, not thinking about You but myself. Please forgive me.

I no longer want to be silent when You have worked a miracle on my behalf. I praise You right now for all the wonderful things You have done for me in my life. I will not keep silent. With Your help, I will move forward, lifting up my voice in the presence of Your children or singing a new song in solitude whenever You rescue me out of a horrible pit—whatever that may be—by Your grace.

I give You my will.

In the victorious, holy name of Jesus Christ. Amen.

9.

Trust In The Lord

September 11th, Labor Day weekend, a few days after the heart transplant interview, I received a call from my health insurance's transplant case worker, Debbie, saying, "Reginald, you've been approved for a heart transplant." *Wow!* We talked for a few minutes about the progress of the process. Shortly thereafter, I received a call from my heart doctor Nisha Gilotra. She shared with me the wonderful news that I had just received from Debbie. I could come in Friday or the following Tuesday. I told her I would see her on Friday.

I was admitted to Johns Hopkins Hospital in Baltimore, Maryland, on September 14. My spirits were up. I was looking forward to hanging out on the fifth floor with Van the man and doing full-time ministry encouraging the patients and their family.

To complete the admission and get to the top of the waiting list, I needed to undergo a biopsy and a right catheter procedure. This time the catheter would remain in place using a "swan." This would allow the doctors to check the health of my heart daily and would give firsthand insight if there needed to be any changes to the medicine. It was also necessary to keep me on top of the waiting list for a heart transplant. However, that didn't take place until a few days later.

After the procedure, I was hooked up to an IV pole with the swan catheter in my neck. I was confined to my hospital room twenty-two hours a day. I was not free to walk the hallways at will. The ministry I was hoping to engage in seemed to be hindered by that catheter.

Mercy! That's not cool. Stay calm, Reg.

Expectations shattered!

BREAKING NEWS!

"Trust in the LORD with all thine heart; and lean not unto thine own understanding. In all thy ways acknowledge him, and he shall direct thy paths" (Prov. 3:5, 6, KJV).

During that week, I was talking to a sister in Christ, Tammy Francois, a dear friend of mine. I was sharing with her my health journey and how God had been sparing my life.

She said, "Reg, you should share your testimony on social media. We need to see and hear more stories of God's miracles working in the lives of His people."

I replied, "I don't know about that, Tammy. I'm not all that excited about it. I'm not tech-savvy, and I dislike being on video, but I will give it some thought."

With Tammy's suggestion, I moved forward to share my story on social media, trusting in the Lord. I would not focus on my inadequacy. I solicited help from my friends, Susan Smith and Wilma Ward, who established my first Facebook page. I used that page to share the very first video from the fifth floor, room 3. Once launched, it got over 10,000 hits on Facebook. I could see the Lord was leading me as I acknowledged Him in all my ways.

As I continued to share on Facebook the story of what was taking place from the fifth floor, it turned into a ministry—"Reginald's Health Journey"—which ministered to patients inside the hospital and folks throughout the country. This bought me joy in my affliction, impacting my attitude toward the positive.

Wounded warrior, child of God—

In your suffering, keep your eyes and ears open at all times to see where God is leading in your hardships, especially when it comes to encouraging others. Don't hold back, even when you may feel that you don't have what it takes to be a blessing to those in need. Lean not on your own understanding; trust God with what you have and use it for His glory. You'll be amazed at what He will do with it. God wastes nothing. You will experience joy in affliction!

God's promise: "God chose things the world considers foolish in order to shame those who think they are wise. And he chose things that are powerless to shame those who are powerful" (1 Cor. 1:27, NLT).

Prayer

El Roi, the God who sees me—

I no longer want to be idle or inactive because of my physical disadvantage. I no longer want to make excuses for not working for You because the pain runs deep inside my brokenness or because I feel I have nothing to offer.

My health crisis no longer defines me. I understand now that You can take my brokenness and do something marvelous with it, knowing it will be a blessing to many others and bring glory to Your name. With Your help, through the Spirit of the living God, I want to be used by You to encourage others—even if it means being positive in my affliction and demonstrating concrete faith in You when I'm not able to do anything else.

I give You my will.

In Jesus Christ's victorious holy name. Amen.

10.

Setback

In November, an infection hit me, causing the doctors to have the swan catheter removed. It also knocked me off the waiting list. That same day, free of my swan, I was free to come and go around the floor as I pleased, no longer bound to my room. This freedom allowed me to meet Jeff on the day of his discharge. I had wanted to reach out to him for a while, but I was bound to the nurses' schedule with the swan and could not connect with him.

However, that day, as I was warming up my food in the family lounge on the fifth floor, Jeff walked into the family kitchen area. We talked for at least a half-hour that morning. Jeff shared many of his health challenges with me—so many that it made my own issues seem small by comparison. I was amazed at how he was holding up, yet I recognized that his pain ran deep. I sensed the uneasiness in his speech the more he talked about his struggles. He knew he might not have much time left to live. My heart ached for Jeff now.

BREAKING NEWS!

"And we know that all things work together for good to those who love God, to those who are the called according to His purpose" (Rom. 8:28, NKJV).

As the conversation continued at the microwave, we talked about the struggles of being so sick. We discussed the anguish of the heavy heart that we bore and the stress that concern for our families put upon us. We talked about Adam's fall and the plight of sin that causes the suffering in this world.

Then we talked about God's grace. Both of us could have been dead and gone by now, but God was still keeping us alive. We talked about Christ's soon return and the promise of no more sickness, suffering, or death. We discussed receiving new bodies and living in the light of God's glory for eternity.

The more we talked about the goodness of God and what awaits us on the other side of this life of turmoil, hurt, and suffering, the more we began encouraging ourselves in the Lord. We were finding joy in our affliction, in the middle of our pain and hurt. By the time the conversation ended, Jeffrey and I were smiling from west to east. We prayed, and I said, "Jeff, I'll catch up with you later on this evening." We departed.

A few hours later, I stopped by Jeff's room to spend a short time with him. He was visiting with his parents, who greeted me with a warm spirit. Before going to my room for the rest of the evening, I left him a book entitled, *Bible Answers*.

Hanging in my room and reflecting on my encounter with Jeff, I recognized the blessings in my setback. I was not currently on the transplant list, but that was okay. If I had had the swan in my neck that day, I would not have had that time with Jeff. God set it up so we would meet, share, and pray together. I am convinced that none of that would have happened if I had not had that infection. I thanked God for everything—even the infection that I caught that released me from my room and took me off the transplant list. That worked together for our good with a divine purpose.

Wounded warrior, child of God—

In every setback, there's a divine purpose aimed through the boisterous storms of the issues of life, working in your favor, that you may not see or understand at that moment. Stay positive and calm. Move forward; always be ready to be used by God in your suffering. Who knows? That setback just may be something God is using to create an opportunity to encourage the wounded with hope and salvation for the very last time.

Jeff's life was cut short due to cancer just a few weeks after we met. I hope to see him in our heavenly home at the second coming of Jesus Christ.

God's promise: "Plant early in the morning, and work until evening, because you don't know if this or that will succeed. They might both do well" (Eccles. 11:6, NCV).

Prayer

El Roi, the God who sees me—

Lord, I am asking for the courage to trust without wavering when I'm met with a setback in my health crisis, knowing that, under frustration, discomfort, or sorrow, You are working to bring about a desired outcome, by using me, in my life or the life of someone else.

I realize nothing goes to waste in Your kingdom—not even in my hurts or suffering—especially when I serve You. Help me find hope in the setback of hardship and see Your purpose working in my favor for my good so that it's not hopeless when my mind is telling me that it is. Heavenly Father, help me stay faithful in serving You.

I give You my will.

In the victorious holy name of Jesus Christ. Amen.

II.

One Hug Will Do

They tell me a person needs seven hugs to get through a day. It may be true in most cases, but every now and then, I believe one hug will do!

One morning, I was not feeling the greatest. My spirit was weighed down watching other patients fighting heart disease and seeing them going in and out of the hospital. I saw post-heart transplant patients with complications, and I began thinking about how my life would be after the heart transplant added to the misery.

> *But the human side was getting the best of me as the negative emotions were running deep.*

Most days, I didn't let it shake me. I knew the God I served could bring me through without significantly reducing my quality of life. But the human side was getting the best of me as the negative emotions were running deep.

On that day, I would receive a text from a dear female family friend affectionately called "Nan" by my two little girls. She was giving my wife a much-needed break by watching after them and was thoughtful enough to send pics of the girls via text. At my first glance upon those pics, my heart felt like it was hit with a ton of bricks! I immediately became aware that my soul longed to be with my girls.

Lord, I'm feeling hurt!

BREAKING NEWS!

"And this same God who takes care of me will supply all your needs from his glorious riches, which have been given to us in Christ Jesus" (Phil. 4:19, NLT).

I had thrown myself into ministry there on the fifth floor. I focused on God's mission while I waited for a new heart. Ministry had been a welcomed distraction from my struggles. However, I missed my girls' laughter, their calls for "Daddy," and their spontaneous energy and silliness with giggles that light up wherever they are. I missed the quiet moments and earnest prayers, rocking them both to sleep in my arms as they sat with me in my chair at bedtime, listening to our favorite gospel songs. I must admit I'm getting teary-eyed now as I write this chapter.

As I was overtaken by sorrow, one of the nurses, Tayna, came in to check on me. Even though she didn't sense my anguish, she offered me a heavenly hug of encouragement. It was as if God, the One who promised, "I will supply all your needs," wanted me to know He'd heard my cry. It lifted my spirits and brought a sense of peace to my troubled heart, even while I was separated from my family. Spending twenty-two hours in a room every day can be overwhelming! He provided what was needed for me to rise above my broken spirit! He sent Tayna to demonstrate His love for me in my affliction.

Wounded warrior, child of God—

As you travel through this journey, when you are overwhelmed with sorrow and your heart is so heavy with pain, remember that God has never left you nor forsaken you. He sees your troubled heart. He knows your needs even if it does not seem that He is aware of your situation. He cares for you. His promise to you is, "I will supply all your needs." Believe His promise with your whole heart. I know it is not easy to do or to receive in the midst of suffering, but you can with the Lord's help. This will bring comfort in your affliction.

God's promise: "I will answer them before they call for help. I will help them before they finish asking" (Isa. 65:24, ERV).

Prayer

El Roi, the God who sees me—

Thank You, Jesus, for being the ultimate provider. A God who is very aware of my everyday physical, emotional, and psychological needs and who will take care of them.

I know there are moments when I find myself impatient, when my situation is not working out in my favor, and when sorrow has settled in my wounded heart bringing grief or taking me to the verge of losing my mind. Help me to remember Your promise that You will take care of all my needs and help me to not lose heart while I wait on You. The journey has been hard, lonely, and long, but I'm choosing, Lord, to trust in You.

I give You my will.

In the victorious holy name of Jesus Christ. Amen.

12.

Life in Songs

November 26, 2018, 10:30 p.m., I was in Jim Evans' room, a fellow heart patient at Johns Hopkins. We were lounging on the sofa, tapping our toes to Kirk Franklin's, "I'd Rather Have Jesus," and Aretha Franklin's, "Precious Lord, Take my Hand," and "Never Grow Old." We were listening to the music, drowning out our worries, lifting holy hands. Our eyes were closed; our heads were rocking side to side.

Mercy, Lord! Indeed, it was a sweet moment! We enjoyed the music while talking about the goodness of the Lord. Masked behind our worship experience, we found ourselves at times still struggling with frustration and uncertainty. Not knowing what the future would hold as we continued this journey, we were both battling against heart failure, trying to stay alive in our foxhole.

"Man, Reggie!" Jim stated, "I'm scared! Tomorrow morning, I'm having quadruple bypass surgery! They're going to cut open my chest. What if something goes wrong? What if I don't make it through the surgery? And, if I do come out of it, certainly there's going to be a lot of pain! The thought of dealing with pain is overwhelming. Reg, I can't tolerate pain. Man! I'm scared!"

BREAKING NEWS!

Jesus says, "The Spirit is the one who gives life; human nature is of no help! The words that I have spoken to you are spirit and are life" (John 6:63, NET).

This passage has always inspired me to keep playing and listening to gospel music. Listening to God's words and His concepts in song gives me encouragement and life. This night was no different. The music positively affected us—especially Jim—since it was the night before his surgery. I have discovered in situations like these that it's easy to talk about politics, family, sports, and your unfavorable situation without ending as distractions. That was not the case on that night.

We kept the music flowing. The atmosphere was so pleasant and full of optimism that it attracted the attention of Jim's nurse and left a great impression upon her countenance as she poked her head into the room from time to time. Jim needed God's strength to sustain him in the pain that was sure to follow. Eventually, Jim talked less about the "what ifs," and he felt less scared. Although knowing tomorrow morning he would lay on the cutting board, undergoing that quadruple bypass, his words turned more to hope, strength, and courage in his affliction.

We continued our fellowship, listening to music and cracking jokes. We laughed and encouraged each other well past midnight. We closed out our time together in prayer, claiming the promise found in Psalms 112:7, "They do not fear bad news; they confidently trust the Lord to care for them" (NLT).

Wounded warrior, child of God—

Be encouraged! Remember there is power in Christian music. The concepts of music that embodies the Word of God can and will speak life into your helplessness. It will generate strength, courage, and resilience to help you persevere in affliction. So go ahead right now and grab hold of some of your favorite Christian music. Allow it to play on until your spirit is lifted above the agony that is weighing you down. By God's grace, you will move forward expecting great things from God, knowing He will take care of you!

God's promise: "Speaking to one another in psalms and hymns and spiritual songs, singing and making melody in your heart to the Lord" (Eph. 5:19, NKJV).

Prayer

El Roi, the God who sees me—

I desire to pursue an atmosphere of holiness that will keep me connected to You in my affliction—especially in the inspirational godly music I listen to that speaks of You, that illumines the spirit within me, speaking life, strength, and comfort in my brokenness.

It reminds me of Your goodness, and Your mercy is with me 24/7. Thank You, Lord, for godly music. I want to experience the joy, peace, and fellowship in You in my suffering that is expressed in the old gospel hymn of Anthony J. Show, "What a fellowship, what a joy divine, leaning on the everlasting arms! What a blessedness, what a peace is mine, leaning on the everlasting arms!"

Lord, I give You my will.

In the victorious holy name of Jesus Christ. Amen.

13.

A Soldier's Testimony: Ms. Wharton

On Thanksgiving Day, I stopped by Ms. Wharton's room to spend some time with her. We were scheduled to record a video testifying about her journey fighting heart disease. We were visited by her 20-year-old daughter, Kennedy, a survivor of cardiac pathology, along with her son, Jason, and his girlfriend, Samantha.

About fifteen minutes into our visit, I started recording the video.

"Good evening, everyone; this is Reggie Reg, the brother man on the fifth floor at Johns Hopkins Hospital in Baltimore, Maryland. We want to talk about the goodness of God. Indeed, He has been good to us. I have Ms. Walton here with me. I want to ask Ms. Walton, won't you explain to us your health condition in relation to your heart?"

She responded, "I've been dealing with a heart disease called 'cardiac pathology' and an overgrown, enlarged heart for the past twenty-eight years. This disease has driven me into depression through the years, knowing that it can shorten my life at any time. It is creating in me the fear of death."

She continued, "You have bad days and good days. Some days, you are always battling. You are in the midst of heavy warfare; you are sick. Most people have the sense of confidence that they will wake up the next day. There are circumstances in which you can definitely lose that confidence. I have been there more than once.

"My thinking was not right. I was depressed! This fear of dying before my time was becoming debilitating, not allowing me to move."

BREAKING NEWS!

"O give thanks unto the LORD, for he is good: for his mercy endureth forever. Let the redeemed of the Lord say so, whom he hath redeemed from the hand of the enemy" (Ps. 107:1, 2, KJV).

Ms. Wharton continued testifying to me about the fear of not being there for her kids, who still depended upon her.

"If I die, they are not ready to live without their mama, even though they are young adults. This added additional stress to the ongoing drama of fighting cardiac pathology."

As I continued to listen to Ms. Wharton, her smile of joy attentively captivated me, and I got excited in my affliction. I shifted gears based on her words of hope and tone of deliverance, which testified about the goodness of God and that the fear of dying early was "no longer an obstacle" standing in the way. It was removed "only by the grace of God." A few years back, I had cried out to God, "I need You to help me with what I can't do on my own. I can't do it."

I was so inspired by her testimony up to this point that I had to interject: "Sister Girl, what I hear you say is that the Lord has delivered you from the enemy's fear of death."

"Yes! Yes! No man knows the time or the hour. The time when I leave this world was written before I was born when I was just a thought."

"Come on, Sis, let the redeemed of the Lord say so" (see Ps. 107:2, KJV).

Wounded warrior, child of God—

When you find yourself fighting negative thoughts of dying before your time and those thoughts are causing depression, shift your mind from hopelessness to controlling what you can to improve your mental health. Take to heart daily that God loves you and has control over the number of your days. Allow this to be your focal point. I guarantee that you will find freedom from this bondage of dying early to experience joy in affliction.

God's promise: "You saw me before I was born. Every day of my life was recorded in your book. Every moment was laid out before a single day had passed. How precious are your thoughts about me, O God. They cannot be numbered!" (Ps. 139:16, 17, NLT).

Prayer

El Roi, the God who sees me—

Wow! What an awesome God I serve! The one who has the whole world in his hands. You remain in control over the affairs that go on throughout the planet. Nothing catches You off-guard—not a single death. Help me find hope and joy in my suffering even when death is present as I think about Your omnipotence, the God who is all-powerful.

With Your omnipresence, as the God who is all-present, and Your omniscience, as the God who is all-knowing, sickness cannot claim my life unless You allow it. You calculate the number of days in my life. Please help me enjoy the present moments each day and not focus on the expiration date. Lord, I want to be found in You when I'm laid to rest because I will live again and experience eternal life.

I give You my will.
In the victorious holy name of Jesus Christ. Amen.

14.

Power in God's Word

December 17, 2018, was a beautiful sunny Sabbath afternoon. I was in my room alone, lying in bed. My spirit was a little down. I had no visitors from my home, the Allegheny East Conference, or patients from the fifth floor.

It seemed it might just be a lovely and relaxed day. But then I heard a knock on the door. Elder William Smith, Evangelist and Publishing Director of the Southern Union Conference, caught me by surprise. I wasn't expecting him. I knew he was in town for business but was unsure that he'd make it up to the hospital.

In less than an hour, I was visited by my brother, Java Madison, pastor and Publishing Director from the South Central Conference of Seventh-day Adventists, and his buddy, hospital chaplain Williams, from Columbus, Ohio. Within about fifteen minutes, there was another surprise visit. It was from my boss, the President of the Allegheny East Conference of Seventh-day Adventists, Elder Henry J. Fordham, III.

Mercy, war horses! The dream team was right there on the fifth floor. My spirit was lifted. I said, "Since all of you are here, let's go to work encouraging the sick." We prayed and headed towards the door into the hallways.

BREAKING NEWS!

"In the beginning God created the heavens and the earth. The earth was formless and empty, and darkness covered the deep waters. And the Spirit of God was hovering over the waters. Then God said, 'Let there be light,' and there was light" (Gen. 1:1–3, NLT).

As we were making our way down the hallways, I decided to do a quick video to encourage the Facebook family, the ex-fifth floor patients who had gone home or been transferred to another floor, and those who were following the journey through social media.

The video began with one of the nurses excited to be recording this event. The ministry was now moving forward. I started by saying, "This is your boy Reggie Reg, the brother man on the fifth floor."

Shortly after, I introduced the group. Next, I asked each one of them to give a word of encouragement, starting with Elder Smith, a warrior prostate cancer survivor less than a few years out, the wound still fresh from the battle. Smith gave us a word about the power of God. The power was so strong!

"Jesus spoke seven words, 'Young man, I say unto you, rise,' and the dead boy came to life.

"He spoke just six words, 'Thy faith has made thee whole,' and a blind man could see.

"He spoke just four words, 'Let there be light,' and the whole universe lit up.

"He spoke three words, 'Lazarus, come forth!' and a dead man who had been dead for three days got up.

"One time He spoke only one word, 'Go,' and six demons had to leave. He said, 'Come,' and a man walked on something that men usually sink in. We are talking about God with all power—resurrection power!"

Mercy! Our spirits were lifted as we struggled to contain ourselves, smiling from west to east, tapping each other on the shoulders. Our walk seemed to be stumbling like we were walking on uneven gravel ground.

The sounds of hymns and "Yes, yes," blustered lightly from our lips as we journeyed down the hallways. God's Spirit was resting upon us. We were fighting in joy in Reggie Reg's affliction.

Wounded warrior, child of God—

Take heart and do not faint, weary one. There is living power in God's Word. The voice that spoke at the beginning of the Creation, "Let there be light," when there was nothing but darkness bathed in its atmosphere of blackness, made light appear. He has more than enough power to sustain you in your suffering, to bring healing in your brokenness, and to keep you in your right mind while the pain runs deep. In your suffering, meditate on God's Word. Believe it, receive it, live it, enjoy it, and experience joy in your affliction.

God's promise: "He sent His word and healed them, And delivered them from their destructions" (Ps. 107:20, KJV).

Prayer

El Roi, the God who sees me—

There is power in Your words to heal me when I'm sick. There is power in Your words to sustain me in my afflictions, power in Your words to keep me emotionally stable in hardship, power in Your words to get my body moving when it says it can't.

There's power in Your words to change a defeated thought into victorious empowerment. There's power in Your words to bring healing to a grieving heart. There's power in Your words to speak hope to the hopeless as they are uttered from my mouth because they are Your words. My Lord and Savior, help me surrender my life to You and drink from Your Word daily to experience that power in my suffering and bring joy in my affliction. Yes, Lord, what an awesome God I serve!

I give You my will.

In the victorious holy name of Jesus Christ. Amen.

15.

The Second Interview

On December 1st, I was visited by one of my dear friends, Mario Broussard, II, his lovely wife Natasha, and his son Declan. The visit was short and pleasant. Less than an hour before their departure, I mentioned to Mario, "Let's do a quick video." He agreed with excitement. So the recording began.

"Good afternoon, everybody; this is your boy Reggie Reg, the brother man here on the fifth floor at Johns Hopkins Hospital in Baltimore, MD. I'm blessed to have you here with me, Mario. Mario is on the Hope Channel's TV program, 'Let's Pray.' It comes on every Wednesday at 8 pm. Mario, what's going on with you, doc?"

"I'm good, Reg. It's good to see you. It's always good to be here. I want to interview you today. You have been here for 75-plus days. Every time I see you, you've got joy in your heart. It is just a testimony to me and so many people. I want to jump right into it. How is it you're able to maintain all this joy and peace in the middle of dealing with cardiac sarcoidosis, something that is trying to take you out of here?"

BREAKING NEWS!

"He will wipe every tear from their eyes, and there will be no more death or sorrow or crying or pain. All these things are gone forever" (Rev. 21:4, NLT).

I started talking about what brings me joy and happiness in my affliction, especially in the trying hours when my heart is heavy. I like to laugh and to tell jokes. It cheers me up. The Bible says, "A cheerful heart is good medicine, but a broken spirit saps a person's strength" (Prov. 17:22, NLT).

"Mario, you want to hear a joke?"

"Yeah, go ahead, Reg."

"When was medicine first mentioned in the Bible?"

"I do not know, Reg."

"When God came down from the mountain and gave Moses two tablets!"

We both laughed. The conversation continued.

"But at the end of the day, Mario, I discovered that when joking and laughter cease, I go back feeling the pain again."

The Bible says, "Laughter can conceal a heavy heart, but when the laughter ends, the grief remains" (Prov. 14:13, NLT).

I look at this cardiac sarcoidosis. This disease is trying to take me out. It has caused me suffering and pain, and I continued to share with him about how the effect of cardiac sarcoidosis may affect my life after the transplant.

"But the good news, at the end of the day, Mario, is that this pain will not last forever! There will be no more death, or sorrow, or crying, or pain in that place called 'heaven.' Paul calls it 'paradise.' John calls it 'the New Jerusalem.' David calls it 'the Holy Hills.' " By the time we got to this point in our conversation, we were rejoicing in my affliction.

Wounded warrior, child of God—

Hang in there by God's grace with a heart of faith, believing that the pain will not last forever in suffering. Do not be overwhelmed by the affliction. By faith, God can give you healing and comfort now in grief while the hurt remains. Life is short in the grand scheme of things. We know this world will end and everything that is part of it—including our pain—with either death or the second coming of Jesus Christ, if we are alive when He comes. Then He will take us to our heavenly home to enjoy peace without pain in our new home throughout eternity.

Yes, Lord, we long to see that day!

God's promise: "Our hearts ache, but we always have joy. We are poor, but we give spiritual riches to others. We own nothing, and yet we have everything" (2 Cor. 6:10, NLT).

Prayer

El Roi—the God who sees me,

I am hurting, and the pain runs deep. At times it can be unbearable. I wouldn't say I like it, and it's causing so much misery here on earth. I wish my suffering would cease. The daily struggles are real; the hardship is wearing out my soul.

Your Bible tells me that heaven is real. There will be no death, no medications, no sickness, and no hospitals there. The Great Healer helps me to fall in love with heaven so my mind can rest there. More than heaven, let me fall in love with You, Jesus; heaven would not be sweet without You. My heart is heavy with grief. Thank You, Lord, in advance that there is a place of hope in glory in the eternal kingdom, where hurt, pain, and suffering will not be part of my vocabulary.

I give You my will.
In the victorious holy name of Jesus Christ. Amen.

16.

Heavenly Atmosphere

December 5, 9:30 am. I was sitting in my recliner, relaxing and listening to gospel music. The room was toasty and very bright from the sun shining through the large windows, making it presence known as its golden presence rose over the city of Baltimore, Maryland.

The team of doctors entered my room, doing their daily rounds, conducting their examinations, and giving me a report regarding the status of my health. They also informed me of any changes that were needed in my medication. The news was the same as the previous day. After their examination, I said, "I got a joke for y'all before you go."

They said, "Okay, let's hear it."

The joke ended, we laughed, and the medical staff moved towards the exit to leave the room. Dr. Sebi, one of my favorite doctors, noticed I had my Bible open to the book of Psalms on my bed and asked my favorite book. I shared that I have many, but there is one that especially means a lot to me now as I travel this path of affliction.

BREAKING NEWS!

"For thou wilt light my candle: the LORD my God will enlighten my darkness" (Psa. 18:28, KJV).

I explained that the candle in this text is David and that God will light him up through the power of the Holy Spirit and cause him to shine for God's glory even in his darkest hours. This was my experience. The last few weeks had been a roller coaster ride for me. I'd been experiencing lots of shortness of breath, major fatigue, fluid build-up, heart palpitations, and irregular and erratic heart rhythms. In the last few days, I went from being able to walk around the halls, as much as I wanted, with the nurses joking about how fast I could get around, to barely being able to do a single lap. It had been quite a challenge.

After explaining the text, I was able to share with them four principles I currently live by:

1. Stay in the Scriptures and claim God's promises.
2. Stay in an attitude of prayer.
3. Do not dwell on the negativity of your situation.
4. Reflect on God's goodness and what He has done for you in your crisis and tell others about it.

I shared that this was my formula for being up in heaven's atmosphere. When you are up in this atmosphere, the Lord will light you up and set you ablaze with His glory.

Afterward, the chief doctor gave me some encouraging words. "I can see that you're living that out here on the fifth floor as we watch you walking around the hallway playing your gospel music and encouraging folks. Your attitude and demeanor are very rare; they are not common at all." Those words brought me joy in my affliction.

> *I shared that this was my formula for being up in heaven's atmosphere. When you are up in this atmosphere, the Lord will light you up and set you ablaze with His glory.*

Wounded warrior, child of God—

We serve a mighty God who is willing to light you up in your darkest hour. When you turn to Him with everything you have within yourself, through prayer, staying positive, claiming his promises, and not entertaining negative thoughts about your suffering but talking about His goodness even in suffering, you will find your darkness overshadowed by the presence of God's Holy Spirit shining in your heart in your affliction.

God's promise: "But the fruit of the Spirit is love, **_JOY_**, peace, longsuffering, kindness, goodness, faithfulness, gentleness, self-control. Against such there is no law" (Gal. 5:22

Prayer

El Roi, the God who sees me—

I'm running to You right now, Lord. I'm going to bypass all the external factors and my putting my trust entirely in them to improve my situation and bring relief. I praise You, God, for the people and medication that You have given me that have helped sustain me on my journey of affliction, but they're not enough. I need more.

I'm still battling fatigue; my poor health that is not getting better; my spirit remains crushed because I'm in this hopeless situation. I need happiness, the heart of hope, and to be patient in suffering as I wait for a breakthrough. Help me, Lord, to remain positive, to talk to others about Your goodness while in hardship and to stay in meditation in Your Word with prayer so that Your Spirit can light me up in my affliction.

I give You my will.

In the victorious holy name of Jesus Christ. Amen.

17.

Struggle to Pray

One evening, I was lying in my bed after finishing my daily walk. I was very tired and my heart felt heavy as my health had just taken a turn for the worse. I began sorrowing because I could no longer walk my usual laps or go flying up and down the hallway while hooked up to an IV pole. Also, I had begun to experience a decrease in the functionality of my voice, and I had no jokes for patients, and I said little to the nurses. The situation became a devastating blow emotionally. It brought me again to the realization that I was dying, and my heart was steadily going out without slowing down.

This emotional weight was weighing me down. Mentally, I was shutting down and fading out. My physical body was becoming weak. I was having a hard time keeping my eyes open, and I struggled to pray. I felt I'd neglected the very One I needed the most. How could I request healing when I failed to give Him the time He desired to spend with me? I felt so guilty. Although in despair and feeling somewhat defeated, I knew that few words were sufficient, so I cried out, "Lord, I need you!"

BREAKING NEWS!

"Moses' arms soon became so tired he could no longer hold them up. So Aaron and Hur found a stone for him to sit on. Then they stood on each side of Moses, holding up his hands. So his hands held steady until sunset. As a result, Joshua overwhelmed the army of Amalek in battle" (Exod. 17:12, 13, NLT).

At that moment, as I struggled to pray, God spoke to my spirit, directing my attention to my Facebook page, "Reginald's Health Journey." I had posted a day or two before, asking the Facebook prayer warriors and my family to pray for the fifth-floor patients and me. The prayers had been coming in for healing and deliverance. "Let them carry you and your problems to the throne of grace when you feel as though you're not able to take yourself." So that's what I did! Immediately, a sense of calm rested over me—I knew that somebody was praying for *me!*

While dozing off to sleep, the Lord reassured me that it was okay to relax and lean on the saints for help when I was in need—even when I found myself struggling to pray for healing. God brought to my mind the story of Moses when he was tired and weak and needed the support of Aaron and Hur to hold up his arms in the battle against the Amalekites. As long as his arms stayed up with the help of his colleagues, victory was guaranteed to the children of Israel. This gave me a deeper level of peace. Before I knew it, I was sleeping like a baby in the Lord.

Wounded warrior, child of God—

When you find yourself struggling to pray to Adonai, the Lord of all, when the heavy burdens of affliction are pressing you down, never forget that you are not alone! Someone is praying for your deliverance on your behalf. As a matter of fact, I have prayed for you. Please allow me to give you another word of encouragement. Our Lord and Savior prayed for your well-being when He was here on earth. So go ahead and rest well in the arms of the Almighty God. He is working in your favor. Trust Him with the outcome.

God's promise: " 'I am praying not only for these disciples but also for all who will ever believe in me through their message' " (John 17:20, NLT).

Prayer

El Roi, the God who sees me—

Thank You, Lord, that You have not left me as an island unto myself fighting in the spiritual warfare when I find it challenging to pray to You, making me feel guilty when fatigue, worries, emotional stress, or some physical health issue are wiping me out.

Please, Lord, in those moments of frustration and weakness when I'm struggling to pray, direct my attention to the prayer warriors lifting their voices on my behalf and praying for me so I can find calmness in their prayers. My Heavenly Father, help me not be discouraged when I'm not always able to spend quality time with You, but let me trust in You, though I have few words to say.

I give You my will.

In the victorious holy name of Jesus Christ. Amen.

18.

Don't Worry

It was around the first week of December that I had the opportunity to visit the room of the Eljuri family from Ecuador. They were a family with whom I had had fun cracking jokes and laughing in the hallway the previous evening during their stay at Johns Hopkins. It was the last night before the discharge of their father, who was experiencing heart challenges and needed a lung transplant. I was there to encourage him and his family through the Word of God and prayer.

That evening was another very emotional experience; the pain ran deep on all sides, affecting the caregiver, the wounded, and me. The connection was genuine. As I shared with them the struggle of dealing with heart failure, I was moved emotionally. During that time, I was trying not to have an emotional breakdown, though overwhelmed by the extra suffering I had been experiencing lately and knowing that my health had taken a turn for the worse. Deep down, my soul cried out daily, "Lord, my spirit needs to be encouraged as I'm encouraging others."

BREAKING NEWS!

"Don't worry about anything, but pray and ask God for everything you need, always giving thanks for what you have" (Phil. 4:6, ERV).

Fifteen minutes into the conversation, I opened my Bible to the passage above: "Don't worry about anything, but pray and ask God for everything you need." We have this privilege because He is our heavenly Father, and we are His children; we have this freedom in prayer. So, by God's grace, try not to get discouraged if you don't receive the very thing you are looking for as soon as we pray. God, our Father, knows what is best.

It's just like the child who asks her daddy for a treat. Sometimes the answer is "yes," sometimes it's "no," and sometimes it's to wait. Just like parents look at the bigger picture before they answer, God, who sees all, looks at the bigger picture of our lives and answers accordingly. Just remember that God loves you and that He has your best interest at heart.

For the next 20 minutes, we continued the conversation. I witnessed a shift in the atmosphere in their tears of joy. There was a calm glow on their countenances, trusting that God can bring about a desirable outcome even if it's not in our timing but His. He knows what's best.

Before I concluded with prayer, the son reminded me of the exact words I encouraged them with; he expressed heartwarming sympathy towards me and my condition and the length of time I had stayed in the hospital. "When you ask God for what you need, our heavenly Father knows what's best. If your prayers about receiving a heart are not answered in your time, wait on God. He has your best interests at heart." Hearing those words again brought relief to my suffering and took me deeper into resting and trusting in God. I began focusing more on the Lord's timing, knowing His timing is always best.

> *You may be amazed in your affliction—the one you seek to encourage may be the one who becomes the encourager!*

Wounded warrior, child of God—

In your suffering, do not remain in an atmosphere of self-pity, feeling sorry for yourself, saying, "Woe is me." This behavior will hurt you emotionally, taking you down into a pit of hopelessness that you may find a challenge to escape. In that place of despair, seek to encourage someone else to take your mind off your suffering. It makes no difference how you do it. You may be amazed in your affliction—the one you seek to encourage may be the one who becomes the encourager!

God's promise: "The liberal soul shall be made fat: and he that watereth shall be watered also himself" (Prov. 11:25, KJV).

Prayer

El Roi, the God who sees me—

Today I'm choosing to serve You by going out and encouraging someone who needs encouragement by an act of kindness even though I don't feel like it. My body is weak, depression is wearing me down, and sadness has taken up residence in my spirit.

I know it will not be easy when my body is telling me to lie down and rest. I need Your supernatural power. I have nothing to give. Show me what You would like me to do: to cook someone a meal or take someone to the store who needs transportation or just call someone on the phone to be a listening ear. I know by Your grace, if I take the first step, encouragement can be found for myself in encouraging others. Help me, Jesus, to move.

I give You my will.

In the victorious holy name of Jesus Christ. Amen.

19.

I Have A Question

One evening my nurse came into my room. It was around 11:15 at night. I was in bed, dozing off to sleep. My gospel music was playing, and the temperature was just right. The bed was feeling nice and cozy. This was not common. That therapeutic feeling was de-escalating the stress of living in the hospital. The lights turned off in the room made it somewhat dark, though not entirely, as the light shone through the blinds on the door from the hallway, bringing a sense of calmness to the atmosphere.

The nurse grabbed a chair from the other side of the room, stationed it next to my bedside, and sat down not too far from where my head was resting. The visit was unique and different; there was no checking of vitals or handing me medication. This was not so much of visitation but simply to see how I was doing or if I needed anything.

"I have a question," she said. "Reg, why do you go to church on Saturdays? I grew up going to church on Sundays, believing it was the Lord's Day. I'm Catholic. Does it matter what day you go to church?"

"Oh yes, my dear Sis. The Lord has a day that the Bible speaks about as being His."

BREAKING NEWS!

"Remember the sabbath day, to keep it holy. Six days shalt thou labour, and do all thy work: But the seventh day is the sabbath of the Lord thy God.... For in six days the Lord made heaven and earth, the sea, and all that in them is, and rested the seventh day: wherefore the Lord blessed the sabbath day, and hallowed it" (Exod. 20:8–11, KJV).

Lying in bed, I did not have my Bible with me. It was on the other side of the room. Instead of turning on the lights, I grabbed my cellphone and turned to my Bible app.

I started with the text to "remember the Sabbath day, to keep it holy …." (Exod. 20:8–11, KJV).

I explained to her out of the seven-day weekly cycle, the only day that the Lord declared to be holy was the seventh day of the week—not the first day, which is Sunday, or any other day in the seven-day cycle. It was the "seventh day"—the Sabbath—that He "blessed" and "sanctified" (Gen. 2:3, KJV). I shared with her that the word "sanctified" means to be set apart for holy use. There were no other days that received that label.

> *"Wow, Reg! It makes sense. It's something to look into. Thanks for sharing."*

We talked about a few reasons why many good and faithful Christians honor Sunday instead of the Sabbath as the Lord's day of worship. Many think they are honoring the day on which Jesus was resurrected, a day that Roman Emperor Constantine officially established in 321 A.D. Others consider the seventh-day Sabbath a Jewish day and not a day for Christians to recognize, not realizing that the seventh-day Sabbath was given to Adam and Eve—who were not Jews—at the beginning of Creation (Gen. 2:3). Abraham is considered the father of the Hebrews, which are Jews.

Looking at the time, I noticed twenty to twenty-five minutes into the conversation that the nurse was getting excited. My spirit was being revived, talking about the goodness of the Lord in my affliction. At the end of the conversation, she said, "Wow, Reg! It makes sense. It's something to look into. Thanks for sharing."

Wounded warrior, child of God—

Do not allow any hardship that you're going through silence your voice. Wherever you are, when you are given an opportunity, share God's Word. We are always encouraged to be ready to provide a reason for our faith and what we believe. It makes no difference what it is. It could be on prayer,

God's everlasting love, or His faithfulness to sustain you in suffering. Just be ready to share. It will have a transformative, positive effect on the listener and on your own emotional well-being in your affliction.

God's promise: "Preach the word of God. Be prepared, whether the time is favorable or not. Patiently correct, rebuke, and encourage your people with good teaching (2 Tim. 4:2, NLT).

Prayer

El Roi, the God who sees me—

It was God who created the seventh-day Sabbath, the day of rest, the only sanctified day, which was set apart for holy use from the beginning of the Creation. Give me Your love. I desire to walk in obedience and to keep Your Sabbath, worshipping You in spirit and in truth on Your holy day.

Lord, I desire to live out Your will in the land of the living. You have done so much for me. Spare my life, giving me salvation through the death of Your dear Son, our Lord and Savior Jesus Christ. Help me to be faithful to Your Word unto death—and not to tradition. Please take me deeper in understanding Your Sabbath and anchor my faith in this beautiful truth.

I give You my will.

In the victorious holy name of Jesus Christ. Amen.

20.

3 A.M.

Around 3 a.m., I was awakened from a deep sleep by the doctor. "We got a heart for you." I was not all that surprised nor excited at the moment, but I was grateful to hear those words once again. Five days earlier, again around 3 am, the same doctor awakened me, "Reg, we may have found a heart, and I stopped by to tell you the good news."

> **"We got a heart for you."**

After the doctor left my room for the second time, I struggled to go back to sleep. I was a little overwhelmed by the news. I didn't want to get too excited because a final examination of this new heart could result in it being rejected due to other issues like the last one a few days before. (Cancer cells were found in the body, though not on the heart.)

The doctor said to call my family, which I did. That morning became very busy with the medical team. The energy and excitement in the room were very high among the nurses, doctors, pharmacists, housekeepers, and kitchen crew, who congratulated me. However, I was still on edge until the final report would come back confirming that it was a 100% go.

BREAKING NEWS!

"Lord, thou hast heard the desire of the humble: thou wilt prepare their heart, thou wilt cause thine ear to hear" (Ps. 10:17, KJV).

The doctor's words were still fresh in my mind a few days later. I'm in a similar situation once again, moving forward with preparation. I was holding back anticipation that this event might not occur as I was moved closer to the time of my actual heart transplant scheduled for 6 a.m. My nurse was checking my vitals every hour. Doctors were coming in with different forms to sign along with the anesthesiologist. My wife and son finally made it down a little after 5 a.m. Nurses came in and out of my room, three to five at a time. I had ten to twelve medical staff members celebrating with my family and me on this special occasion. No bad news yet was good news. I was starting to feel confident that this was the day.

I decided to stop by the room of a heart patient named Brian Douglas to let him know. By this time, I was confident that the procedure was moving forward. Our conversation was interrupted by one of the nurses.

"Reg, it's time to go. Two nurses from the heart transplant surgery team have arrived, and they're ready to take you down."

I made it back to my room, jumped into the wheelchair, and my spirit was lifted up. Within myself, I was feeling like David. "Lord, Thou hast heard the desire of the humble." As I was being pushed down the hallway towards the operating room, my wife videoed the experience live on Facebook. I thanked everyone for their prayers and support that the Lord heard our prayers for me to be out by Christmas. I thanked the medical staff for their hard work on my behalf, helping me to stay alive. The last words I said were, "I'll see y'all on the other side. Peace."

> **The last words I said were, "I'll see y'all on the other side. Peace."**

Wounded warrior, child of God—

When uncertainty seems to be present, will God answer my prayers? Let me encourage you—He does. Try not to be consumed with doubt but always stay in the spirit of humility, walking in obedience with a heart of faith in hardship, trusting Jesus as you keep moving forward, and lifting your voice to Him in waiting until you receive the very thing you have been praying for. By God's grace, you shall receive. The Lord hears the "desire of the humble." Bless His holy name!

God's promise: "Now this is the confidence that we have in Him, that if we ask anything according to His will, He hears us" (1 John 5:14, NKJV).

Prayer

El Roi, the God who sees me—

I'm now seeing that prayer is a vital component in staying connected with You, the God in charge of the universe and everything else that takes place under the sun. I'm excited to see that I can come to You and ask You for anything I need and that I can be specific with my requests. It is acceptable to ask and set a time when I would like to see the petition answered.

My Jesus, give me Your humble spirit. I do not want to get prideful when I recognize things are moving in my favor. I love to keep our communication clear without the distraction of pride that will hinder the blessings coming from You. Lord, I thank You in advance for what You are going to do for me. I will keep praying and expecting You to come through for me at the right time.

I give You my will.

In the victorious holy name of Jesus Christ. Amen.

21.

When My Voice was Silent

As I entered the operating room, the lights were bright and the atmosphere was very chilly. The first thing I laid my eyes on was the cutting table. I realized that I'd be lying across that table pursuing open heart surgery in less than a few minutes. A moment later, one of the nurses asked if I was ready.

"Yes," I replied.

"Are you able to walk to the table?"

"Yes!"

A nurse or two were standing by my side. I got up, made my way to the table, and lied down on my back. Immediately nurses were hooking me up to an IV line and placing patches on my body with wires running into different monitors.

Things were moving so fast with medical staff all over the place running in and out of the room. I was in constant conversation with the staff, even cracking jokes. The medical team was pleasant and exhibited care in making me feel comfortable through the prepping procedure.

"Reg, how are you doing?"

"Great!"

"We are going to give you 'sleeping medicine' through this mask."

"Come on now! Give me some of that good stuff!" I said.

"Relax, and breathe in and out. Count down to one, starting with ten, nine, eight, seven, six, five ..."

By this time I was sending up a short prayer.

"Lord, get me through this procedure. If not, remember me at Your second coming."

I went out.

BREAKING NEWS!

"And you are helping us by praying for us. Then many people will give thanks because God has graciously answered so many prayers for our safety" (2 Cor. 1:11, NLT).

> *"Lord, get me through this procedure. If not, remember me at Your second coming."*

I didn't realize that within the hours of the procedure, my life was on the line even more than usual. I discovered this a few months later during one of the follow-up visits with my surgeon, Dr. Ahment Kilic. During the operation, he said, I was "fighting primary graft dysfunction, a life-threatening event that 4–10% of patients go through during a transplant," he explained. "Your body kept rejecting the new heart, not allowing both sides to work." This situation caused the medical team to go into overdrive, trying to fix the problem so I could stay alive. The surgeon and his team had thought for a moment that I might not make it due to a few complications. As the fight continued, by God's grace, they were able to get both sides of my new heart working.

In reflecting on this event, I realized that there were a few factors working in my favor, such as the medical staff, current medicine, and technology. However, I can't overlook the fact that God was answering the prayers of my "Reginald Alexander My Health Journey" Facebook family and the saints and family who all prayed for my safety as the primary graft dysfunction tried to claim my life without their even realizing what was going on. Here are a couple of their comments:

"His story is transcending. He has no idea of the number of people praying for him. We care and wish the best." –Adelina Nuñez, retrieved from Facebook, 12/17/18.

"Father God, thank You for the kind family who shared in their time of grief—now please be the Chief Surgeon and may this offering not be in vain!" –Denise Johnson, retrieved from Facebook, 12/17/18.

I praise God now in my affliction while writing this chapter in tears, knowing that voices of praise were lifted up with my prayer right before I fell asleep. "And you are helping us by praying for us" (2 Cor. 1:11, NLT). Thank You, Lord, for the prayers of the saints and medical staff. The Lord pulled me through! Wow, Lord, I'm finding joy in affliction in my reflection!

Wounded warrior, child of God—

Move forward, wrestling with the Lord in critical situations with prayer. Do not hesitate to solicit prayers from the prayer warriors. Invite them to be part of the process. You do not have to fight your battles on the journey alone. The good news is that God does answer the prayers of the saints. What do we have to lose? Prayer works. We have this hope, grounded in the promises of God. By His grace, He will have mercy on us, granting us the desires of our heart.

God's promise: "The effectual fervent prayer of a righteous man availeth much" (James 5:16, KJV).

Prayer

El Roi, the God who sees me—

Thank You for the amazing and beautiful prayers of the saints. This is a wonderful gift that You have given to Your children—especially in times of need. Help me embrace this beautiful gift daily in my affliction that I may find hope, encouragement, and strength now and for the next battle I will face. I do not want to be controlled by the fears of the unknown and their devastating effect in time of war.

I want my thoughts to be consumed with the attitude of prayer and more prayer. Heavenly Father, can You help me pray more for others as I try to pray? Teach me to lift up my voice from the heart of faith and lean on the ministry of intercessory prayers from the saints.

I give You my will.

In the victorious holy name of Jesus Christ. Amen.

22.

Dark Shell

After the procedure, while my chest was still open, a balloon pump was connected to my heart. The heart was not functioning at its full capacity. The surgeon, Dr. Ahment Kilic, visited my wife and son in the waiting room and shared that he and the other doctors "didn't know how sick I was." In other words, I was not out of the woods yet. I was still battling the primary graft dysfunction.

I found myself living in a dark shell, resting in the CICU room from the surgery. I was unable to speak or open my eyes, but I could hear. I was sedated and in a coma-like state. I could hear the conversations among the doctors and the nurses walking in and out of my room. My wife read from the book of Psalms and prayed over my life daily.

In that week, Marcellus Robinson, a colleague in ministry, stopped by to visit, giving my wife a break for a few hours. He was sitting at my bedside, holding my left hand. Now and then, after seeing my body jerk, he would ask, "Reg, are you alright?" The only form of communication I had at that time was squeezing his hand. He didn't realize I was undergoing a spiritual and physical battle in that dark shell.

Demonic forces were telling me, "You are not getting up out of here; you are going to die." Daily, these words were wearing out my soul. I don't want to die! I felt like I was losing my mind!

BREAKING NEWS!

"I had fainted, unless I had believed to see the goodness of the LORD in the land of the living. Wait on the LORD: be of good courage, and he shall strengthen thine heart: wait, I say, on the LORD" (Ps. 27:13, 14, KJV).

The battle continued in a dark place for the next few days. Marcellus was gone, and my wife continued to read the book of Psalms. Her prayers would bring a little relief and calmness to my restless spirit. Overall, I felt like I was losing my mind. I heard gospel music playing in my head nonstop. I had no control to turn it off in those moments I craved quiet and rest. I didn't realize my wife was playing it on my cellphone!

> *As I waited on the Lord, I rehearsed those words, "You will live, not die," until the day of my release.*

I was constantly seeing bloody organs. *Mercy, Lord, help me!* I found myself losing my grip emotionally; my spirit was like a raging sea. *Lord, is it true?* I continued to pray and claim Bible promises. Somewhere within those few days, the Lord spoke to my spirit: "You will live, not die."

In that moment of suffering, my mind reflected on one of my favorite passages: "Be of good courage, and He shall strengthen thine heart. Wait, I say, on the Lord." I believed with all my heart as David did when he was facing death, running from his son Absalom, "I will see the goodness of the Lord in the land of the living." Instead of fainting or giving up, my spirit became calm in my affliction. As I waited on the Lord, I rehearsed those words, "You will live, not die," until the day of my release. I opened my eyes a few days later. Within a few seconds, I shared with my wife that I had been in the toughest battle of my life while in this dark shell.

Wounded warrior, child of God—

Even when prayer, Scripture reading, and inspirational songs are present, it sometimes seems not to give complete peace for which you are looking. Hang in there the best you know how. God will speak to you in a small, still voice amid commotion and noise. In those times of crisis, He will speak words of hope customized only for you like He did for the prophet Jeremiah, for Isaiah, and for King David in their times of anguish.

Receive it, without doubting. Trust in His promises. You will find calmness and peace in your affliction.

God's promise: "The Lord of Heaven's Armies has spoken—who can change his plans? When his hand is raised, who can stop him?" (Isa. 14:27, NLT).

Prayer

El Roi, the God who sees me—

It is hard to hear Your voice speaking to me when I'm going through so much agony. This pain makes it difficult to listen to You, especially when my suffering seems to be unfair. I have tried to study the Bible to hear from You. I have listened to inspirational songs and have even prayed at times, but I have found little or no comfort searching for an encouraging word that will hit home.

Lord, I know You are still speaking, and I have been slow to respond to Your voice and embrace it with little or no faith because of my lack of trust in You. Jesus, give me another word that is customized for me, and by God's grace, I will receive it, believe it, wait in it, and find peace in it. As I wait for the fulfilled promise.

I give You my will.

In the victorious holy name of Jesus Christ. Amen.

23.

Cardiac Arrest

Two weeks out from surgery, I am lying in bed. My body is still weak and in pain and stiff, and I am unable to get in and out of the bed to move around. I have fifty pounds of fluid buildup in my body. The room is well lit. The door is open, and I can hear the traffic out in the hallway. It seems very busy. The TV is off, and there is no cell phone within reach to play my favorite gospel music to calm down my anxiety. The post-transplant experience is becoming overwhelming.

Without warning—out of nowhere—doctors and nurses rush into my room. I am slowly fading out. Someone's hands are on my chest. I can hear a lot of commotion, though I don't understand what is being said. What is taking place seems blurry, and the room looks unstable. My attendants place a patch on my chest. Next, they are turning me over, with no resistance on my part. My body is fragile as they place another patch on my back. Things are moving so fast. "Reg," they say, "this is going to hurt."

> **"Reg," they say, "this is going to hurt."**

"Huh, oh," utters from my mouth as the pounding starts and continues. The pounding stops, and I am out!

BREAKING NEWS!

"You saw me before I was born. Every day of my life was recorded in your book. Every moment was laid out before a single day had passed" (Ps. 139:16, NLT).

I am alert—barely—and I am awake. My mental capacity is not functioning at a satisfactory level. I am not fully aware of what has just taken place. I hear the doctor chattering with others; they mention a pacemaker.

I cannot remember if the conversation I was hearing was before or after they put in another pacemaker connected to the new heart. Sometime after surgery, the doctors shared with me that I went into cardiac arrest, experiencing complete heart blockage. The new heart just stopped. How could this be? The heart is strong and healthy. I had not given much thought to what had happened. I was under a lot of pain, stress, and suffering. But I was just happy to be alive in the midst of grief.

As I reflect on the journey that day, I am aware that the devil has been trying to take my life throughout this fight with cardiac sarcoidosis. I am fully convinced that he cannot have my life unless the Lord gives it to him. My life and its length are in the Lord's hands. He saw this day "before I was born. Every day of my life was recorded" in His book (Ps. 139:16, NLT). The fear of death is losing its hold on me lately as I experience joy in affliction while releasing my burden into the hands of God daily. I'm living on God's time, not under the devil's terms.

Wounded warrior, child of God—

Take heart and know the Lord has you in the palm of His hand. Not a single day has passed without His caring for you—even in affliction. The devil is not in charge of your life. He does not set the time for you to live or die. God does. If the Lord has to lay you to rest prematurely, let it be well with your soul in the grief. Do not carry this burden alone. Release it to God and pray, asking Jesus to keep you safe from the enemy of your soul. By God's grace, He will bring hope and peace in your affliction.

God's promise: "But I trust in you, O LORD; I say, 'You are my God.' My times are in your hand; rescue me from the hand of my enemies and from my persecutors!" (Ps. 31:14, 15, ESV).

Prayer

El Roi, the God who sees me—

You have been so gracious to me throughout my life. You have allowed me to see this day knowing that I should have lost my life a long time ago. I recognize that You control my life and the devil cannot take my life without

Your consent. Keep me, Jesus, in the palm of Your hand daily. Help me to relax and focus on You and not be consumed with thoughts of whether I will be in the land of the living tomorrow.

Thank You, Lord, for life, grace, and mercy. I'm moving forward trusting in You. By Your grace, I will never leave You nor forsake You as long as I have breath in my body. Help me to remember that You will get me through.

I give You my will.

In the victorious holy name of Jesus Christ. Amen.

24.

How Long, Lord

It was three weekends after my heart surgery. I was lying in bed frustrated and felt I had doubted God by complaining to Him. My recovery hadn't improved and even seemed to get worse. How long, Lord! I'm not getting healed. I want to get up and walk around. I want to eat real food. I'm thirsty. I just want a cup of water. I want to go home.

I was being fed through a nose tube. I had heavy, shallow breathing that kept me up for days, and it was challenging and painful getting in and out of bed. It was in this context that Dr. Van Whitfield, "Van the Man," a heart transplant recipient and sarcoidosis warrior, stopped by. We were both on the fifth floor together, waiting for a heart transplant. I began to share my feelings with him that I had let God down and that I had doubted God by complaining.

Van said to me, "You did not let God down, Reg. You just went through a lot. God sees and understands your situation while you're under heavy medication."

I was lying in bed, out of it, a little delusional, trying to stay calm and relaxed as our conversation continued. A lot was going on in my head. *Lord, I'm still hurting!*

BREAKING NEWS!

"The Lord is like a father to his children, tender and compassionate to those who fear him. For he knows how weak we are; he remembers we are only dust" (Ps. 103:13, 14, NLT).

I was still lying in bed, cuffed to the bed rails because they were afraid that I would remove the nose tube again for the fourth time. I could not move my hands, and my legs remained in the same position for long periods of time. My body fluids built up, weighing me down. I was still trying to find complete comfort in Van's words amid wrestling with doubting God and the depression that was getting the best of me. We kept talking, and Van kept encouraging me. His visit was brief. Van understood that I was exhausted and unable to say a lot because he had gone through a similar experience as a transplant patient. He was recovering as well. It had only been a few months since his procedure.

Shortly after Van left, my self-pity was overshadowed by the sadness of my doubting God. I began to think about what Van had said, "God knows your situation; you did not let God down." At that moment, the Spirit of God brought the text from Psalms to my mind, giving me a deeper comfort. "For he knows how weak we are; he remembers we are only dust." I began to encourage myself in the Lord, reflecting on that passage along with the words Van had spoken to me. God knew I was frail and weak, and He knew me outside and in. Out of frustration, it seemed that I had let God down, but inside, He knew my devotion to Him was still alive in my grief. "But the Lord weighs and examines the motives and intent [of the heart and knows the truth]" (Prov. 16:2, AMP). Knowing this brought me joy in my affliction.

Wounded warrior, child of God—

When your emotions get the best of you in your trials, it does not mean that it is you. Feelings will come and feelings will go like the four seasons. They are not dependable, nor do they determine who you are. What is in the heart—your devotion to God—outshines your doubting spirit in the presence of our heavenly Father, who is "tender and compassionate to those who fear him." We serve a great God. Give God praise in your affliction.

God's promise: "There is therefore now no condemnation to those who are in Christ Jesus, who do not walk according to the flesh, but according to the Spirit." (Rom. 8:1, NKJV).

Prayer

El Roi, the God who sees me—

Lord, there are moments when I come to You in prayer with a request for healing based on Your command. When the prayer request is not granted, my attitude towards You is that of frustration and disappointment. I feel that You don't care about me. At times I question Your existence or power to heal. Yet, I know You are real.

I am asking forgiveness for those moments I've disappointed You, for not trusting and believing in You while I was waiting for healing. I'm happy to know that my inappropriate behavior does not disqualify me from being a child of God, and I'm sorry for my behavior. Help me, Lord, to accept Your forgiveness without ongoing guilt and help me to not doubt You again in my affliction.

I give You my will.

In the victorious holy name of Jesus Christ. Amen.

25.

Bound!

About two weeks before my heart transplant, Dr. Wills visited me. We had become good friends during my stay there at the hospital on the fifth floor. I was studying Mathew 11:28–30, where Jesus was talking about taking up His yoke.

"What are you doing?" he asked.

"I'm studying the book of Matthew, chapter 11, verses 28 to 30, and I would like to share it with you."

So, we began to look at the text together, pulling out gems and nuggets.

About two weeks after the transplant, Dr. Wills came by checking up on me to see how I was doing and to let me know that he had been following my report. He said, "Reg, you have been through a lot." I had become quite delusional and I had complained a lot about suffering, which seemed to be getting worse.

On top of that, my hands were tied to the bed because the medical team worried that I could potentially hurt myself due to my mental state. I had already pulled out the nose tube three times. I didn't like being restrained or bound to the bed. I repeatedly asked for my hands to be released. I felt like I was losing my mind. The doctor kept telling me, "No!" This caused me to become more and more combative. Man! I was frustrated!

> *I didn't like being restrained or bound to the bed. I repeatedly asked for my hands to be released. I felt like I was losing my mind.*

BREAKING NEWS!

"Come to me, all of you who are weary and carry heavy burdens, and I will give you rest. Take my yoke upon you. Let me teach you, because I am humble and gentle at heart, and you will find rest for your souls. For my yoke is easy to bear, and the burden I give you is light" (Matt. 11:28–30, NLT).

Dr. Wills asked me: "Do you remember the passage we looked at together where Jesus says, 'Take my yoke upon you'?"

"Yes, take His yoke . . . I can't do it."

He said, "Lean on Jesus, and He will carry you through this."

Imagine him saying that to me!

I wanted my hands to be released so badly at the time. I was not happy with what he was telling me.

I said, "Maybe God has sent you to take up the yoke to release me from being tied down."

"No, God wants you to lean on Him."

I must admit I was angry with him and with my wife, who was present in the room, because they would not help. Shortly after he left, I had no other choice but to lean on Jesus and wait patiently until the doctors released me. His positive thought of inspiration brought little rest to my weary soul in affliction.

Wounded warrior, child of God—

I know it can be challenging at times to carry your burdens in hardship, especially when the journey seems to be a long, tough road to travel and when the weight is wearing you down to the point of collapsing. But don't quit. Keep moving forward, grabbing hold of His strength by faith through a Bible passage that speaks to your issues in suffering. Believe that He is there with you, for He is; rest in Him, not in your strength. You can do this with His help. You will find rest in affliction.

God's promise: "Humble yourselves, therefore, under God's mighty hand, that he may lift you up in due time. Cast all your anxiety on him because he cares for you" (1 Peter 5:6, 7, NIV).

Prayer

El Roi, the God who sees me—

Can You teach me to lean on You and place the weight of worries, pain, impatience, and all my anguish on You? Taking up Your yolk will make my affliction a little lighter when times are tough, when the journey seems so long and when it seems like there's no resting place.

As I am working on relinquishing control of my situation to lean on You, Jesus, I want peace and rest, and I want the distress and hurt to go away. I'm claiming the promise in Your Holy Bible right now as the first place to start this process as I wait for the healing: "You will keep in perfect peace those whose minds are steadfast, because they trust in you" (Isa. 26:3, NIV).

I give You my will.

In the victorious holy name of Jesus Christ. Amen.

26.

Come On, Dad. You Can Do This!

I remember one morning, after being in the CICU for three weeks, a physical therapist walking into my room and saying, "Let's go, Reg. Sit up! It's time to walk."

My wife had just stepped out of the room, leaving only my son by my side. I got to be honest and tell you, I did not want to move from my position—lying on the bed, flat on my back. I could barely get up to stand, even with assistance. In the last few days, I had struggled to take even three steps. My body was weak; my energy was at a record low. Forty to fifty pounds of extra fluid had built up in my body, and my bones were stiff and fragile. All of this was accompanied by constant aches and pains. I was hooked up to a breathing device and dealing with pneumonia that would not leave. In my mind, being confined to the bed twenty-two to twenty-three hours a day was the best thing for Reggie Reg, but the medical staff thought differently.

"To get rid of the extra fluids, to strengthen your bones, to get you out of the CICU and up to the tenth floor for recovery, Reg, you need to walk so that you can go home. So, let's go!"

"No, I don't feel like it," I replied, annoyed.

BREAKING NEWS!

"Two people are better off than one, for they can help each other succeed. A person standing alone can be attacked and defeated, but two can stand back-to-back and conquer" (Eccl. 4:9, 12, NLT).

Shortly after arguing with the physical therapist, I decided to sit up, stand, and take that walk in my room with his help, as painful as it was. My legs were shaking and flopping around as I grabbed hold of the IV pole for balance. The physical therapist was holding me up on both sides as I took the first few steps. With those steps, I was in constant pain, moaning and groaning. But it was a success! I managed to walk from my recliner to the door and take over ten steps that day!

"Reg, look at you!" my therapist said. "You've come a long way in the past few days. You can turn around and go to your bed or sit in your chair. Or do you want to move forward?"

I responded, "Let's move forward."

We did a few more steps in the hallway, turned around, and made it back into the room where I "jumped" into the bed, wiped out. Before leaving the room, the therapist gave me a new name, "Spaghetti Legs."

> *"Dad, you can do this! Come on, Dad! Get up, let's go!"*

What motivated me to move and comply, to give in that morning? Was it because I wanted to go to the tenth floor, hasten the time to go home, or strengthen my bones? No, it was the sound of my son saying, "Dad, you can do this! Come on, Dad! Get up, let's go!" I do not know if my son realized it or not, but he embodied the passage, "Two people are better off than one, for they can help each other succeed." His encouraging words that morning brought courage and inspiration in my affliction into that room. It allowed him to witness me take the most steps I had taken since coming out of surgery. We were not defeated that day! We both came out as conquerors, along with my physical therapist.

Wounded warrior, child of God—

When you find yourself in a physical crisis where you don't feel like doing anything, when you have no motivation, your energy level is low, and fatigue is getting the best of you, relax and breathe. He will send someone to bring inspiration to you in your affliction. It may be through family members, friends, or even through medical staff. Or it may be this book that you're reading right now, encouraging you to "Come on now, my dear friend! You can do this with God's help!" Thank the Lord right now in your affliction that you're not alone. I'm right here with you cheering you on. Better yet, the Holy Spirit is with you now as well.

God's promise: "And I will pray the Father, and he shall give you another Comforter, that he may be with you forever, even the Spirit of truth" (John 14:16, 17, ASV).

Prayer

El Roi, the God who sees me—

On this journey in affliction, sometimes I feel lonely—like I have no one in my corner to lean on for encouragement. It is possible that someone is there, but I don't seem to notice because I'm so dazed by what's going on. I am suffering, and I cannot see or hear the cheerleaders in my corner. Lord, give me spiritual hearing and sight to embrace the support You have given me through the medical staff, and through my family and friends to accomplish the task you have set before me.

Heavenly Father, I praise You now in advance for the additional overall support You will send my way and the support I already have. I thank You for being here with me now through the power of the Spirit of the Living God as a Comforter cheering me on.

I give You my will.

In the victorious holy name of Jesus Christ. Amen.

27.

Encouragement in the Foxhole

I was now on the tenth floor, no longer in the CICU. It was the recovery floor, the last stop of residency before going home. My body was still weak and in a lot of pain. I was still having trouble eating, cutting my food, and holding my silverware. I had dealt with blood clots in my bladder, and I had experienced bladder spasms for two-and-a-half weeks. Blood clots were jamming the tip of the foley catheter, causing pain when urinating. I was constantly moaning and groaning. The pain became unbearable.

People could hear me outside of my room. I had lost so much blood from the bladder that I had to receive a blood transfusion. The thought of going to the restroom brought on daily depression. It was disheartening that I did not have enough strength to raise myself off the commode or clean myself after using the bathroom. I always needed some assistance. I was still dealing with pneumonia in my right lung and a damaged diaphragm, making it difficult to breathe. I cried out, "Why me, Lord? Why have you allowed me to be hit with cardiac sarcoidosis that has caused all this suffering? Will I recover?"

BREAKING NEWS!

"Then the king commanded, and they brought Daniel, and cast him into the den of lions. Now the king spake and said unto Daniel, Thy God whom thou servest continually, He will deliver thee" (Dan. 6:16, KJV).

I was in an emotionally distraught atmosphere with not much to say when the team of doctors came by to visit me. One morning, the team showed up in my room while I was sitting in my recliner. They were doing their usual morning rounds, examining patients, and giving reports. Since the surgery, one of the biggest concerns had been my respiratory issue. They had not been able to get my fast, shallow breathing under control. This brought frustration to both parties devoid of answers, not knowing that my left diaphragm had been damaged during my surgery. This issue was revealed a few days later from a pulmonology test.

With sadness on their countenances, they were unable to release the suffering that I was going through. In those moments of the visit, I believe the Spirit of God moved upon Dr. Smith's heart. "Hang in there, Reg. You will get through this. You know the 'Man upstairs.' He will get you through this." I immediately responded with two thumbs up but no words.

> **You know the Man upstairs–He will get you through this.**

These words from Dr. Smith brought joy in my affliction when all else failed. They were words of comfort—reassuring me by pointing to the Great Physician and letting me remember that this too shall pass. Shortly after leaving Johns Hopkins Hospital, reflecting on this experience. I rehearsed the words of my doctor in my head. "You know the Man upstairs–He will get you through this." I could not help but think about King Nebuchadnezzar's words to Daniel right before he was put into the lion's den: "Thy God whom thou servest continually, he will deliver thee." Thank You, Lord, for having mercy on me and bringing me through.

Wounded warrior, child of God—

Stay strong and humble. It's okay to cry in your affliction when it becomes so overwhelming. You are a human being with emotions that can reveal your need for the Lord's help. Do not be ashamed to cry to the Lord when the pain and suffering run deep. This is where you are now. Remember the words that my doctor shared with me in distress. "You know the Man upstairs–He will get you through this." Keep serving Him in the hurt and in the sorrow. By His grace, you will experience joy in affliction.

God's promise: "Overwhelming victory is ours through Christ, who loved us" (Rom. 8:37, NLT).

Prayer

El Roi, the God who sees me—

I praise You, Lord, for who You are, and I thank you for sparing my life throughout the years and for allowing me to see this day. You have been kind and gracious to me in my sickness, even though it has been hard to deal with—from going in and out of hospitals and all the doctor's visits, the never-ending taking of toxic medication and dealing with their side effects, and the daily coping of depression, anxiety, and physical and emotional pain that, at times, have left me speechless.

I will struggle, and when the situation seems hopeless, You will remind me I have someone to lean on upstairs in the heavenly courts. That is You. You will get me through.

I give You my will.

In the victorious holy name of Jesus Christ. Amen.

28.
Wisdom in Season

9:30 a.m. I was lounging around in my office a few months out from being in the hospital. I decided to return a call from one of my mentors in ministry, Elder Alvin Kibble, the Vice President of the North American Division of Seventh-day Adventists. He's also a cancer survivor who suffered a lot, to the point of death.

I'm no idiot when it comes to talking to individuals with great wisdom. I listen more and talk less. I withheld my physical, emotional, and spiritual experience from him. I didn't mention the turmoil that I went through shortly after surgery living in the CICU or how I questioned and doubted the power of God because healing was not coming fast enough when I prayed.

> He said, "Reg, there are moments in our suffering when we will not always have super faith, and that's okay!"

I was still grieving over my past failures and questioning God's power to heal while in the CICU. I don't know why the guilt remained. I should have been completely liberated from that emotional weight weighing my consciousness down. I have believed and embraced His promise: "If we confess our sins, he is faithful and just to forgive us our sins, and to cleanse us from all unrighteousness" (1 John 1:9, KJV).

Not free entirely, the guilt remained my companion.

****BREAKING NEWS!****

"So then faith cometh by hearing, and hearing by the word of God" (Rom. 10:17, KJV).

I remained attentive to his encouraging words, as if he knew my pain and my distress during those days in the hospital when I doubted God's power to heal me. He said, "Reg, there are moments in our suffering when we will not always have super faith, and that's okay!" It is an indication that we need more faith. In those situations, we find ourselves trying to hold onto the little faith we do have. So, when this happens, we must turn to the Word of God! Faith increases by "hearing, and hearing by the word of God."

Mercy! What inspiration in my season of grief—when I was going through so much hardship emotionally, physically, and spiritually, reassuring me that it was okay not to beat myself up emotionally and spiritually when I come up short, doubting God's power to heal me in suffering and that there is an antidote to having little faith in the crises by assimilating God's word! That will raise our trust level in His power either to heal me or to sustain me in my suffering. In my current affliction, I found liberation and joy in those words that morning, in my remorse over letting God down in CICU. What an awesome God we serve! Bless His holy name!

Wounded warrior, child of God—

- Do not let your past failure of doubting (or your present doubting, if you are there) in God's ability to fix your problems get the best of you. Do not torture yourself with the words, "I am unworthy." Stop rehearsing the event after you have repented. You are still worthy because you are God's child! You have been forgiven! You need more faith at this moment to dive into the Word of God. Faith comes from hearing, hearing from the Word of God. You will experience an increase of faith, hope, and joy in your affliction.

God's promise: "But then I decided to confess my sins to the LORD. I stopped hiding my guilt and told you about my sins. And you forgave them all! *Selah*" (Ps. 32:5, ERV).

Prayer

El Roi, the God who sees me—

Thank You, Lord, for the emotions of doubt and for complaining about Your power to heal. These are indicators that there's still growth that needs to take place in suffering. Help me trust in You when I wrestle with these emotions and the guilt that is taking up residence in my heart.

Help me to not allow guilt to become a focal point that consumes me but, rather, that it redirects my mind to study the Bible and meditate on Your promises, increasing my faith in You and Your power to heal. Lord, I'm in doubt with You right now. I am sorry; forgive me. Please give me more faith in You.

I give You my will.

In the victorious holy name of Jesus Christ. Amen.

29.

Purpose in Brokenness

The road has not been easy these past four years, dealing with heart failure, cardiac sarcoidosis, respiratory issues, and the anxiety of living with a heart transplant. The last two years had me intensely diving deeper into the subject of suffering. I tried to make sense of this from God's perspective. By studying God's Word and reflecting on testimonies of others regarding how I impacted their life on my journey, I have become persuaded that everything will be alright. I'm operating in the will of God. It has encouraged me when I have read and heard statements like these:

"Brother Reginald, you're a shoulder to lean on and the voice we hear in the wind." Derek Jones, Sarcoidosis Warrior, Facebook, July 12, 2019.

"You need to hear the gospel according to Reggie Alexander: you need to know what the Lord has done for him!" Elder Alvin Kibble, NAD Vice President of the Seventh-day Adventists.

"They say that there is a reason for everything and that each person is placed strategically to serve a purpose. I believe you were carefully chosen to join our unit (Johns Hopkins) to teach us how to remain faithful in challenging situations." Nurse Sherrell Apugo, December 5, 2018.

BREAKING NEWS!

"But I would ye should understand, brethren, that the things which happened unto me have fallen out rather unto the furtherance of the gospel; so that my bonds in Christ are manifest in all the palace, and in all other places; and many of the brethren in the Lord, waxing confident by my bonds, are much more bold to speak the word without fear" (Phil. 1:12–14, KJV).

These words of encouragement have revolutionized me in my affliction as an ex-cardiac sarcoidosis warrior now living with a new heart. They bring about a change in behavior for good, when I do not feel sorry for myself as I continue to press forward on the battlefield.

Elevating my mind above the suffering, I had to endure His divine plan and look through His spiritual eyes, not mine. I have come to understand this imprisonment, fighting cardiac sarcoidosis, surviving its death-hold, and living with many health challenges that came with having the disease. "That the things which happened unto me have fallen out rather unto the furtherance of the gospel" (Phil. 1:12, KJV).

The Lord used me to encourage the fifth floor family medical staff and the heart failure warriors with their family and friends in the foxhole at Johns Hopkins Hospital, inspiring the sarcoidosis troopers on the battlefield to keep on hoping and trusting in God and reminding them that He has not forsaken them in suffering. He is there to give hope to your family as a living testament that God can heal sickness and keep you in your right mind under the dark storms of affliction. Lastly, God of all comfort used me as an instrument to stimulate a greater spirit of gratitude in saints of God for what they do have in their affliction when they do not have everything they want.

You see "Reggie Reg" on Facebook, YouTube, TikTok, or offline as you continue to follow the journey of my ups and downs. There are no sad faces, just amens and hallelujahs. I have embraced this jacket that the Lord allowed me to wear in my health crises as a divine assignment, recycling the affliction of cardiac sarcoidosis for His glory. It has been an honor to serve the King of the universe in this capacity, which has brought joy even in affliction.

Wounded warrior, child of God—

My friends, stay encouraged and share your story! The suffering you're going through now and that you have gone through is not in vain. Your "suffering is never for nothing" (Elisabeth Elliot). Someone needs to hear your testimony that God is sustaining you in your affliction. He can take your tragedy and put it through a divine recycling process by the Holy Spirit to be used for His glory and to further the gospel and encourage someone else. That will bring life and purpose to your broken spirit and body through His Son Jesus Christ. That, my friends, is God's love in your brokenness. He is with you in your suffering. You are not alone.

God's promise: "For I know the thoughts that I think toward you, saith the Lord, thoughts of peace, and not of evil, to give you an expected end" (Jer. 29:11, KJV).

Prayer

El Roi, the God who sees me—

I embrace my new assignment in affliction. I pray, Jesus, that You use me in a way that will bring honor and glory to Your name.

Lord, let my work be reviving to those who are going through a trial. Allow my testimony to be a blessing to my family. At the end of the journey, when all is said and done, may my prayer be to hear those words from You at Your second coming, "Well done, thou good and faithful servant: thou hast been faithful over a few things [suffering and witnessing], I will make thee ruler over many things: enter thou into the joy of thy Lord" (Matt. 25:21, KJV).

I give You my will.

In the victorious holy name of Jesus Christ. Amen.

Reflections

God Speaks

"The heavens declare the glory of God; and the firmament sheweth his handiwork. Day unto day uttereth speech, and night unto night sheweth knowledge. There is no speech nor language, where their voice is not heard" (Ps. 19:1–3, KJV).

Friday night, August 13th, around 10:30 p.m., I awoke. My mind was restless, and I was unable to sleep. I made my way to my brown leather recliner located in my living room to do some writing. Leaning back in my brown leather chair, trying to get relaxed with my phone in hand and notebook app open, I began writing on the text. "The heavens declare the glory of God; and the firmament sheweth his handiwork ..."

Meditating on the text, I got up from my chair and made my way towards my bedroom. *Lord, I need to hear from You.* "Day unto day uttereth speech, and night unto night sheweth knowledge." As the dark night overshadowed my bedroom, I began to visualize the billions of stars, the never-ending galaxies, and the moons roaming throughout the open solar system.

Wow! What a loving God I serve, with so much power and creativity! While my mind was elevated, thinking about the solar system He created, the God of creation spoke to my spirit, reminding me, "I got My eyes on you. You are going to be okay as long as you abide in Me." He is with me! Once again, I found joy in my affliction as I climbed into bed. "There is no speech nor language, where their voice is not heard."

Sometimes, servants of God, we must behold the glory of God in His handiwork. Herein the Lord speaks to us, giving us a more profound revelation of who He is.

A Safe Place

"Lord, you have been our dwelling place in all generations. Before the mountains were brought forth, or ever you had formed the earth and the world, from everlasting to everlasting you are God" (Ps. 90:1, 2, ESV).

There's not a day the Lord does not think of you and me. We're always in His presence, and His eyes watch over us continually, especially the born-again believer. We have nothing to fear about what is happening now nor about what will come in the future because, "Lord, you have been our dwelling place in all generations." And He still will be until the end of the world.

Have you surrendered your life to Christ? Are you walking in obedience to His will? Do you love Him? If so, trust in His promise without wavering or complaining about His being there with you. Jesus says, "If anyone loves me, he will keep my word, and my Father will love him, and we will come to him and make our home with him" (John 14:23, ESV).

What an awesome God we serve! He loves us and will dwell within us. When I think about that evening, it brings joy to my affliction! What about you, my friend? We can abide in Him in whom is peace, intimacy, joy, and holiness—in a God who existed "before the mountains were brought forth"—and can pray, "From everlasting to everlasting You are God."

We have a safe place we can call home. All who give their life to Jesus are welcome.

Free Gift

"The fear of the LORD is the beginning of wisdom: and the knowledge of the holy is understanding" (Prov. 9:10, KJV).

Each night before tucking my two little girls, Eden and Brooke, into bed as my custom, we kneel at one of their bedsides to begin our evening prayer and Bible reading. One Sunday night, right before bedtime, I was blessed to have another opportunity to enjoy a great worship experience with them, sharing the text, "The fear of the LORD is the beginning of wisdom."

I asked the girls, where does fear come from? Brooke said, "God wants us to be afraid of Him." I, too, held this viewpoint at one time. What about you? Thankfully, I found out from studying the Bible throughout my journey with Jesus that God desires my love, respect, and sincere worship without my being afraid of Him. "For God hath not given us the spirit of fear [being afraid], but of power, and of love, and of a sound mind" (2 Tim. 1:7, KJV).

The spirit of fear, or being afraid, is birthed out of our fallen humanity. It causes anxiety, hopelessness, and separation from God. However, the fear God desires for us to have, is what Paul calls "godly fear" (Heb. 12:28, KJV). Such is the fear of the Lord. It is given to us by Him as a free gift. "I will put my fear in their hearts," the Lord says, "that they shall not depart from me" (Jer. 32:40, KJV). Thank You, Jesus!

If this wonderful gift, the fear of the Lord, is received, it will reconcile us to God, bringing true wisdom, respect, love, and peace—even in our affliction.

His Everlasting Love

"The LORD hath appeared of old unto me, saying, Yea, I have loved thee with an everlasting love: therefore with lovingkindness have I drawn thee" (Jer. 31:3, KJV).

I'm extremely grateful that I serve a God who changes not. He loves us with an everlasting, unconditional love. His love doesn't fade in and out when we fail, nor does it carry an expiration date. It remains steadfast with perseverance overlaid with care and ongoing affection. Can you believe this, child of God?

There were moments in my affliction when I questioned Jesus' love for me, and I did not feel His love in my grief. I was frustrated at times—especially when the suffering seemed to have no end. In the valley of affliction these past few years, I have become increasingly convinced that His love is a principle—not a feeling—revealed in action. No longer a theory, it's the real deal!

He loves me even when I don't feel it in my affliction or when all my wants are not being met. He has not forsaken me. His lovingkindness is still active, holding me up in hardships, sustaining me in the land of the living, and meeting all my needs. I am forever grateful for this principle in action and every blessing I receive from Him in suffering. His love is drawing me—but not just me, child of God, His love is drawing you too!

In the midst of trials, what blessings can you find in your life that demonstrate God's everlasting love when the feeling's not present?

He Never Stops Leading

"When I am overwhelmed, you alone know the way I should turn. Wherever I go, my enemies have set traps for me" (Ps. 142:3, NLT).

I praise God this evening that we have an Everlasting Father full of insight. He is in our corner 24/7, and He is highly acquainted with our infirmities. Throughout the ages up to this present time, the Lord has always been there with His children—especially when their spirit is crushed.

This evening, if we were conversing about suffering over a nice meal, would you talk about those times you have experienced unrest, not knowing what to do in your crisis? Perhaps that is where you are right now. I know it can be a nerve-wracking adventure in your stressful moments void of answers and solutions. I have been there. Relax your troubled mind and breathe. You're still on good grounds, my friend, in Christ.

Be encouraged in your affliction as you journey through the valley of uncertainty, not knowing what to do next. "Trust in the LORD with all your heart; do not depend on your own understanding. Seek his will in all you do, and he will show you which path to take" (Prov. 3:5, 6, NLT). He alone knows the way you should turn (Ps. 142:3, NLT).

Wait quietly and patiently for the answers you need. The Lord is just a whisper away. He will never stop leading you.

About the Book

- Are you going through a health crisis that has left you physically handicapped and emotionally suffering with low self-esteem?
- Do you wrestle with the feeling of loneliness and the thought that no one cares about you in your affliction?
- Have you lost hope in God's love for you because your health crises are stripping away your quality of life?
- Do you ever wonder, *Does God have a purpose for me in my affliction?*
- Are you longing to experience happiness and joy despite your challenges?

If so, this book is for you! Be inspired by the Word of God and the author's personal testimony. Journey from asking, "Why me, Lord?" to discovering joy in your affliction. Short, power-packed daily devotional thoughts, birthed from the pain of bitter experiences and disappointments, deliver encouragement in your times of need.

Each devotional chapter shares a clip from the author's personal story, interjects a Spirit-filled break with a message of hope, and concludes with a prayer of rededication. Wherever you may be on your journey, this book will help you grow closer to the God who cares. Discover (or rediscover) absolute joy in affliction.

"My health may fail, and my spirit may grow weak, but God remains the strength of my heart; he is mine forever" (Ps. 73:26, NLT).

About the Author

Reginald Alexander is an ex-cardiac sarcoidosis patient who now lives with a new heart. He is a full-time licensed missionary leader in evangelism employed by the Allegheny East Conference of Seventh-day Adventists. He enjoys writing, teaching, preaching, equipping, and empowering church members—especially those going through health crises—to become soul winners for Christ. He is the founder of Joy in Affliction Ministries and is an author and motivational speaker. He lives in Pennsylvania with his two little girls, Eden and Brooke.

Author's Website: www.JoyinAffliction.org
Facebook: Joy in Affliction

Lord, it's hard not to feel overwhelmed when experiencing all kinds of emotions ... when I'm going through hard times. These feelings of suffering can lead me to ask, "Why me, Lord?" as I become absorbed in my trials. But thank you, Jesus, that I do not have to remain in a hopeless state. I am not alone. Your eyes are on me. Lord, help me to remember this in my affliction and help me to believe that You are active in my suffering even when Your voice seems to be silent, and Your invisible hand cannot be seen in my grief. Help me to remember that You will get me through.
I give You my will.
In the victorious, holy name of Jesus Christ, Amen.

TEACH Services, Inc.
P U B L I S H I N G

We invite you to view the complete
selection of titles we publish at:
www.TEACHServices.com

We encourage you to write us
with your thoughts about this,
or any other book we publish at:
info@TEACHServices.com

TEACH Services' titles may be purchased in
bulk quantities for educational, fund-raising,
business, or promotional use.
bulksales@TEACHServices.com

Finally, if you are interested in seeing
your own book in print, please contact us at:
publishing@TEACHServices.com
We are happy to review your manuscript at no charge.

www.ingramcontent.com/pod-product-compliance
Lightning Source LLC
Chambersburg PA
CBHW072031170426
43200CB00025B/2552